Postliberal Theology

A GUIDE FOR THE PERPLEXED

Postliberal Theology

RONALD T. MICHENER

B L O O M S B U R Y
LONDON • NEW DELHI • NEW YORK • SYDNEY

Bloomsbury T&T Clark

An imprint of Bloomsbury Publishing Plc

50 Bedford Square
London
WC1B 3DP
UK

175 Fifth Avenue
New York
NY 10010
USA

www.bloomsbury.com

First published 2013

© Ronald T. Michener, 2013

British Library Cataloguing-in-Publication Data
A catalogue record for this book is available from the British Library.

ISBN: HB: 978-0-5675-1899-6
PB: 978-0-5670-3005-4

Typeset by Fakenham Prepress Solutions, Fakenham, Norfolk NR21 8NN
Printed and bound in Great Britain

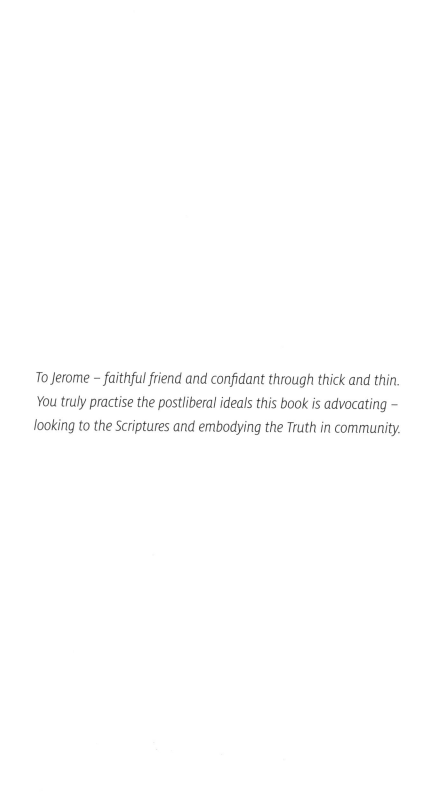

To Jerome – faithful friend and confidant through thick and thin. You truly practise the postliberal ideals this book is advocating – looking to the Scriptures and embodying the Truth in community.

CONTENTS

CHAPTER 1

Introduction

We live in an era where the mighty prefix of 'post' reigns in the academy. We have postcolonialism, poststructuralism, post-Marxism, postmodernism and also postliberalism. Perhaps these designations speak to a mentality that is more self-reflective on history, maintaining a vision to move beyond the past without ignoring it and at the same time learning from its failures. To be *post*modern is to *remember* the modern, recalling its technological victories, yet reprimanding its reductionism. The postmodern thinker realizes that reducing life to progress, technological or otherwise, via empiricism and rationalism, will never result in the utopia that much of modernism's proponents seemed to promise. The designation of the prefix 'post' at the very least implies that we must not forget that to which the 'post' refers. If we are thinking in postcolonial categories, we must never forget the abuses of the imperialist past of colonialism. The past must be understood in part in order to understand the present, so that we make right decisions about the future. While acknowledging the past and giving it critical reflection, these complex terms have seemingly developed a life of their own. As a result, some of these modes of description now used in highbrow discussions are doomed to remain in the ivory towers. But this should not be the case for *postliberal* theology.

The proponents of postliberal theology would have us bring its convictions into the life of the church, not simply into sermons, but into the flesh and blood of everyday people – with a vision to see thriving communities of faith and practice. When it comes to the 'post' in postliberal theology, it is absolutely not 'post-church,' even though it is certainly post-apologetic, arguably post-conservative and certainly postmodern. It is towards understanding the context and background of this compelling pro-church movement to which we now turn.

What is postliberal theology?

What is postliberal theology? At first glance, one might think it pertains to the various theological developments following classic theological liberalism represented by Friedrich Schleiermacher, Adolf von Harnack and Albrecht Ritschl, among others, dominating the modernism of early twentieth century theology. This is partially correct, as the prefix 'post' appears to suggest. However, postliberal theology is significantly more focused that its mere etymology betrays. It is both postmodern and premodern. It calls us to move beyond the historicism and rationalism that set the agenda for modernist religious thought, calling for a return to a premodern faith rooted in the faith community, while fully realizing the impossibility of a full return to premodern dogma.[1]

The agenda of classic liberal theology rode naturally on the coattails of the Enlightenment and its succeeding modernist agendas. Modern advancements in science, history and philosophy resulted in the demythologization and demystified leveling of the Christian faith into moral kernels of timeless love and truth. This was not an abandonment of Christianity, but a serious reworking and redefinition of its language and pre-critical paradigms. Miracles and science simply do not mix, so a modernist apologetic agenda for the Christian faith needs to dig below the supernatural grammar of the biblical world to discover the universal concepts existentially relevant for humans in today's world. This is one direction.

Another more conservative orientation (as we will spell out more clearly in the next chapter) also takes the rational and empirical demands of modernism seriously, but rather than jettison all things seemingly supernatural, one must rigorously defend and justify all faith commitments and propositions using the methods and suppositions of the rational and empirical. This conservative approach has unfortunately led to some negative tendencies among

groups associated with Christian fundamentalism or evangelicalism. Some tend to view scripture as a collection of propositional
spiritual vitamins: verses to be read each morning for a burst of
spiritual energy to carry one through the day. The Bible is seen
more as a collection of holy snippets, rather than a narrative
of God's work in and through His people throughout history.
Spirituality and evangelism in this model often become activities
of verbal assent to certain commonly accepted propositions, rather
than activities of the heart and body involving change of character
and radical love for others. In its effort to remain true to the
onslaught of modernist demands, both liberal and conservative
approaches end up being drained of the vitality of the Christian
faith in community.[2] Postliberal theology is introduced as a *tertium
quid* solution between these perceived extremes of modernism and
propositionalism.

Postliberal theology, especially in terms of its origins, has often
been associated with what is called the 'Yale School,' referring to
former Yale Divinity School professors, most notably, Hans Frei
and George Lindbeck. Indeed, this has some merit. But if postliberal
theology depends solely on Yale for its existence, then, as George
Hunsinger notes, 'postliberal theology is in trouble'. As we will see,
it is a broader movement than its professorial advocates from Yale.
Postliberal theology has always been more a loose connection of
narrative theological interests than it is some monolithic agenda.
It represents an overarching concern for the renewal of Christian
confession over theological methodology.[3] Rather than reliance on
a notion of correlative common experience, postliberal theology
moves toward the local or particular faith description of the
community of the church.

The 'postliberal' to which we will be referring in this book
will always be theological or philosophical in focus, rather than
political. Within the study of theology itself, another distinction
must also be made. When used as an unhyphenated word,
'postliberal,' it will refer to the movement discussed in this book.
The hyphenated form of the word 'post-liberal' refers to an earlier,
historically specific neo-orthodox rejection of classic theological
liberalism during the years before and after World War Two. This is
not to say that there are no common threads between the historical
situatedness of 'post-liberalism' and the later 'postliberal' critique
of liberal theology as developed by Hans Frei, George Lindbeck

and others. Both *post-liberal* and postliberal theologies reject efforts to modernize Christian doctrines to make them palatable to contemporary scientific or rational mindsets. Both are concerned with the retrieval and maintenance of classic Christian doctrines and practices of the Church. Nevertheless, due the historical context, the nuanced differences among the authors, along with current postliberal insights with respect to postmodernity, we believe that making this distinction between the two is important to maintain.[4]

Descriptions and characteristics of postliberal theology

This rich and diverse movement of postliberal theology cannot be simply defined. But this we know for sure: it always stresses the narrative of scripture along with the community of the church and its practices. With efforts to provide a more complete description, we will discuss several of the common characteristics of postliberal theology that surface in the writings of its proponents. We will look specifically at characteristics given by William Placher and Hans Frei, while also providing commentary on these themes in dialogue with additional authors.[5]

There are a variety of ways to describe and divide these sometimes overlapping and interconnected themes of postliberal theology. On reflection, we suggest that there at least five basic themes or characteristics representative of the various expressions of postliberal theology:

1 It is non-foundationalist.
2 It is intra-textual.
3 It is socially centred.
4 It respects plurality and diversity.
5 It embraces a generous orthodoxy (i.e. it is ecumenically focused).

First, postliberal theology is non-foundational in its epistemological understanding. There is no assumed neutrally detached, unbiased or ahistorical foundation for uncovering knowledge through rational or empirical investigation. With modernity, the drive was to sift through our traditions and religious trappings to get to a common human core of understanding. The challenge of pluralism, in some respects, simply solidified this perspective. Rather than embracing the particularity of our religious roots and faith communities, we generalized them all for the sake of harmony. Instead of truly recognizing diversity, all religions become flattened out, reduced to different ways of seeking the same God, supreme force, or ultimate reality. For the postliberal theologian, this ethical reductionism is neither possible nor desirable. There is no 'ultimate' common ground or foundation that we should seek either in religion or in our philosophy of knowledge. A universal, objective rationality is simply unattainable. Further, it ignores a basic aspect of our humanity: our differences.

The postliberal submits that our deep embeddedness in our particular cultures, backgrounds and traditions has deeply shaped and coloured our entire worldviews and perspectives. But this is not seen as something we should try with zeal to abandon, rather, it is something we must guard and cherish. With postliberal theology, the revelation of the Christian faith is a *particular* commitment to a *particular* narratival understanding of reality. Understanding that all systems of knowledge and reality are deeply rooted in community and culture is what opens up the door for the postliberal voice. As Alister McGrath observes: 'With the end of the Enlightenment and its intellectual satellites – including liberalism and pluralism – the embargo on distinctiveness has been lifted.'[6] For the postliberal, rather than promoting universality and the levelling of difference, difference and particularity are embraced as the means by which reality is made accessible.

Postliberal theology does not look for its credentials outside its own faith narrative structure, neither does it believe we should. Simply conceding all notions of truth and reality to the pervasive human propagated knowledge paradigms of modernism is wrong-headed. Too often Christians have 'bought into' a positivistic view of our Christianity that looks more toward a justification of modernism's call for 'facts' (that is, 'facts' according to modernist agendas) instead of turning to the faith and tradition of the Christian narrative. This is why postliberal theology also avoids a systematic approach to apologetics and tends to avoid systematic theology.

Since it is opposed to proofs based on empirical or rational foundations, it turns to ad hoc, contextualized approaches for examining
the claims of Christianity. At the same time, it acknowledges that
we already bring ad hoc assumptions to our theological expressions
– but we must resist the temptation to continually put them into a
system. It does not allow faith to be shortcircuited by empiricism.
Instead, postliberal theology unabashedly affirms the distinct and
particular character of Christianity, which has its own language
and meaning within the context and practices of the church.[7] In
this regard, it desires to remain distinctly and specifically Christian
in both its method of inquiry and its subject of inquiry.

A second theme that emerges from the first is that postliberal
theology is inherently 'intratextual' rather than extra-textually
centred. A postliberal theological vision absorbs all reality into
the story of scripture, the church, and more particularly, the story
and life of Jesus. As mentioned earlier, the grammar of all life
and thought emerges from the praxis of the church. Rather than
trying to make scripture fit the story of modernist ambitions and a
rationalistic secularism, scripture creates and sustains a world of its
own from within which the community finds its ability to believe,
to reason, and to maintain its identity. This being said, it does not
follow that the world of the Christian is completely isolated from
the pluralistic world in which it finds itself. Instead, Christians
draw on the narrative of the Bible to make sense of the world in
its diversity while maintaining the particularity of the Christian
faith.[8] Stanley Hauerwas expresses this well when he states that the
theologian's task is not making the 'gospel credible to the modern
world, but *to make the world credible to the gospel*'.[9] If we work
from the world to the relevance of the gospel, we will continually
compromise the gospel narrative for the sake of relevance. If we
begin with the narrative of scripture, the ever-changing world will
find its place in the gospel of God. The Christian faith has value
in its own merit and language; it does not need support from the
'outside' in order to be justified. It is *post*liberal in that it does not
look exclusively or primarily to either experiences, on one hand,
or to propositions, on the other. It is not that these are totally and
necessarily excluded, but they are not the primary means by which
the Christian faith is expressed.

There is a parallel that is often made to grammar in postliberal
theology that is significant for our understanding not only in terms

of illustration, but in actual practice. Grammarians do not sit in centres of learning and invent languages, create communities by which a particular language may be used, then make the rules that govern that language. Likewise, for postliberal theology, doctrines were not simply constructed by theologians who then, in turn, formed communities that were willing to believe and apply these doctrines. When someone learns a foreign language, it is best accomplished not by simply poring over the rules that have arisen governing the language, but rather by immersion within a community that speaks the language. The rules of the given language have arisen in the context of community practice. It is not that the rules communicate nothing, but apart from the community, they do not provide the best means by which to truly absorb the language and its context. William Placher provides the following example that deftly illustrates this:

> If I go to my pastor, I don't want just psychological counseling – I can find someone better trained in that elsewhere. And if my pastor has only the language of contemporary psychology with which to help me think about my life, then he or she has no alternative to the better-trained psychologist down the street to offer. In short, Christians don't seem, in a variety of contexts, to function well as Christians if they let various contemporary languages take over the discourse of their communities.[10]

Likewise, learning and understanding the Christian faith in terms of its discourse and grammar requires immersion in the community of faith. Just as with communities speaking a particular language, it may that only few within the church community are able to formally articulate their own grammar or doctrines, even though the 'rules' are more or less consistently followed in community practice.[11] Doctrines arose within the practice of the early Christian community. Many were, in fact, developed and articulated ad hoc at various periods and official councils of the church in response to divergent perspectives that (at least) appeared to be proposing (and/or practising) elements contrary to the traditions and practices of the broader church community at that time. We say this not to give an estimation on which doctrines were always correct or incorrect, but simply to make a general statement on how they contextually arose.

Moreover, the rules that govern one language do not necessarily govern, neither may they be imposed, on another. The rules of French grammar cannot be imposed on that of English or German. It is due to this perception of incorrigibility that postliberal theology is often harshly criticized as isolationist. Of course, simply because all rules of grammar for a particular language may not be applicable to another does not necessarily imply the lack of applicability to all rules and functions of grammar. Furthermore, it also does not preclude the impossibility of some sort of partially meaningful conversation between those of different language groups. Philip Kenneson points out that if part of the basic grammar of the church is about being reformed but always seeking reformation (*ecclesia semper reformanda*), then it may still be conversationally relevant to those outside its particular faith context.[12] We will come back to this thought more specifically in a later chapter.

A third predominate theme in postliberal theology (that is probably obvious at this point), is that it is socially and communally centred. The radical individualism that characterizes much of modernist thinking is repudiated by postliberalism. The self as an autonomous individual that determines, plans and thinks its own course of being and action is radically challenged. Instead, our thoughts, identities and understandings are always mediated through our communal contexts and relationships. Identity is revealed through cultural, historical, and linguistic contexts. This aspect of postliberalism marks it as truly postmodern. Where modernism is completely caught up with the ideals of the self, individual freedom and the potential for progress, postmodernism effectively challenges this entire enterprise of the self-contained individual.[13] This is not to say that all modernist impulses discount community on all fronts, but the stress is heavily centred on the individual itself, rather than looking towards how the individual fits into the community. Postliberal theology is concerned about the community first, where the place of oneself within that community is secondary.

Accompanying this theme of community is the postliberal emphasis on narrative or story. We are members of a community of faith, but the local community is only a part of a larger narrative of the working of God in and through His people throughout history. We are a part of a larger community of the people of God that is carried out in the narrative of the past, present and future. Indeed, postliberal theology stresses the community of faith expressed in the particular community, but the community is not merely local, privatized and self-contained. Our particular story in the local community is part of an ongoing story of God's narrative in scripture. Hence, we do not change the scripture to fit modern ideals, we keep to our faith-history narrative *as it is* while consistently asking how modernist ideals either fit or do not fit with this narrative.

A fourth theme in postliberal theology is that it respects plurality without affirming pluralism. We alluded to this theme earlier in our discussion of postliberalism's non-foundationalist epistemology. Although often accused of isolationism, postliberal theologians are open for interreligious and cross-denominational dialogue. But the goal is not to try to get the 'lowest common denominator' behind the religious particulars and differences in order to form some universal religious foundation (pluralism), but rather to sincerely acknowledge religious differences (plurality). At the same time, this does not imply that all differences are equally embraced as teaching the same core reality. Respect and recognition of genuine religious particulars in the course of dialogue does not mean that all beliefs are accepted as 'true' by the dialogue partners.[14] Mutual respect in the course of dialogue does not imply mutual belief and commitment.

A fifth predominant theme of postliberal theology is the concern for a 'generous orthodoxy'. This is a term that has become popularized in recent post-conservative evangelical circles, but the term is borrowed from Hans Frei.[15] As we have said, postliberal theology turns away from liberal theology and the demands of modernism, seeking the recovery of orthodox faith. For Frei, this means that we must learn to read the biblical narrative where, as readers, we are a part of the biblical story. William Placher applies this by challenging us to embrace an ecumenical faith immersed in history, through the works of Aquinas, Luther and Calvin. But we do not engage history in a vacuum – we have a critical eye for insights and application as we consider and reconsider our own cultural contexts that shape our theological and ecclesiological margins.[16] This does not mean we reduce our particularities for a shallow ecumenism, but we embrace an ecumenism to refine, correct, and shape our particular faith expressions with an acknowledgement of the broader, diverse community of faith now and throughout history.

Postliberal theology and theological 'types'

Robert Andrew Cathey suggests another approach to understanding postliberal theology 'on its own terms' besides looking
at its primary themes, is to consider the five types of Christian
theology discussed in Hans Frei's posthumous work, *Types of
Christian Theology*.[17] In each of these types, Frei begins by
identifying the particular theologian who is representative of the
theology he is describing. He uses these characteristic 'types' to
provide a broad spectrum of Christian theology, in order to show
where his version of postliberal theology fits on this spectrum. So,
we will briefly consider each of these types given by Frei, while
remaining in dialogue with both Cathey and David Ford. We will
begin with types one, two, and three, then move to number five,
while concluding with number four, the type that is associated with
postliberal theology.

For the first type of theology, which Frei associates with Gordon
Kaufman, theology is seen as a discipline of philosophy for
'conceptual or imaginative construction'. In this type, Christianity
is reduced to a part of the universal, rational quest for reality that
is simply part of the history of Western culture. This theological
type represents the height of modern hubris with its seemingly easy
dismissal of the supernatural and unreserved embrace of modern
rationality.[18]

The second type of theology is represented by David Tracy's,
Blessed Rage for Order, in which Christian theology is viewed as
phenomenological philosophical reflection on common human,
internalized experience. David Ford suggests that Rudolph
Bultmann would also fit into this category. Bultmann believed that
existentialist philosophy provided insights on the nature of human
existence as seen in the New Testament. The heart of the Gospel,
apart from its mythological trappings, allows us the opportunity to
embrace freedom to trust God in the midst of life's insecurities.[19]

Frei suggests that the third type of theology is that represented
by Friedrich Schleiermacher. Schleiermacher is concerned with how
Christian self-description is related to its external descriptions.
Theology must not be simply reduced to academics; for there is
a correlation between Christian self-description in the Church
and academic theology. Theology is a second-order language that

reflects the first-order language of the general human condition of the feeling of absolute dependence. Of course, as Ford points out, Paul Tillich would be the classic representative of the method of correlation. Tillich's concern was to correlate faith with culture by showing how significant symbols of religion can answer the fundamental questions about the meaning of life. For example, the symbol of God as Creator can help provide us with meaning if we are faced with life's devastating problems. The main idea with the method of correlation is to continually walk between faith and culture, without letting either one take over.[20]

The fifth type of theology is an attempt to recreate the reality of Christianity as expressed in Scripture, disregarding modern worldviews and philosophies. Frei associates the Wittgensteinian philosopher D. Z. Phillips with this view. For Phillips, theology is the internal language for religion. It is not that philosophy is subservient or secondary to theology; it is simply a completely different discipline, with only internal criteria of sufficiency.[21] Philosophy or science cannot be the judge of theology; likewise, theology cannot be the judge of disciplines outside its own field of inquiry.

The representative for the fourth type of theology is the primary 'background' theologian of postliberal theology: Karl Barth. Frei claims that Barth finds the 'heart' of theology in the ongoing dialectic between the 'first-order' language of Christian discourse from the Bible and confessions of faith along with their 'second-order' redescription. Barth has no pretensions about attempting to correlate theology to other disciplines or build a theology or systematic apologetics from natural theology. Instead, Barth looks to his understanding of all reality and Christian doctrine from the standpoint of the narrative of the Bible, which inspired Frei's similar notion of absorbing the world into the story of Scripture.[22] We will consider Barth further in the following chapter when discussing the theological background to postliberal theology.

Thus far we have attempted to simply identify the basic characteristics of postliberal theology by looking at five basic themes that emerge in its writings. Second, we turned to Hans Frei's proposed types of Christian theology to discover not only what postliberal theology is not, but to suggest which type is most closely associated with the various emphases of this broad movement. We trust this synopsis will be helpful to provide a basic framework from which to proceed. Next, we will provide some reflections on the origins and received contexts of postliberal theology, followed by our stated goals and overall plan for this book.

Origins and reception

Although the origins of postliberal theology undoubtedly stem from the United States, it has progressively found its place among English-, German- and French-speaking theologians as well.[23] As German theologian Bernhard A. Eckerstorfer, OSB, remarks:

> While the debate concerning his proposal was slow to ignite in the German-speaking world, it has in the meantime become a reference point in German Catholic fundamental theology. Lindbeck's controversial book might even cause further discussion in Europe, following the publication of the French translation in 2002.[24]

Due to postliberal theology's postmodern critique on theological liberalism and conservative religious fundamentalism alike, it was not difficult to move the debate into the context of northern Europe that has encountered similar theological strains, albeit in different cultural and religious contexts. It was Karl Barth (again, we will note more specifically later) who provided the theological call away from theological liberalism for a return to the centrality of scripture and the church. His influence is unmistakable with regard to the central moves of postliberal theology and its concern with the recovery of tradition and the communal character of the Christian faith. One may argue that postliberal theology is the Anglo-American modification of the European French Catholic *nouvelle théologie* seeking a *ressourcement* or return to original sources of Christian faith for constructive help to challenge the demands of modernism.[25] Modernist theological liberalism declared that via the rigours of human reason and experience, we might obtain objective, neutral, universal truth, regardless of the culture or context of the individual. In doing this, liberal theologians accommodated Christianity to these modernist assumptions and demands. Instead, postliberal theology argues that the Christian faith must be accepted on *its own* terms, rather than forced to fit into a secular mould, absent from the narrative of scripture.[26] Although we believe he presents a caricatured over-generalization of the differences between European and American views of epistemology, Slavoj Žižek provides an interesting analogy that illustrates the postliberal attachment to community and tradition in contrast to modernism:

> In Europe, the ground floor in a building is counted as 0, so that the floor about it is the 'first floor,' while in the US, the 'first floor' is on the street level. In short, Americans start to count with 1, while Europeans know that 1 is already a stand-in for 0. Or, to put it in more historical turns: Europeans are aware that, prior to start counting, there has to be a 'ground' of tradition, a ground which is always-already given and, as such, cannot be counted, while the US, a land with no pre-modern historical tradition proper, lacks such a 'ground'—things begin there directly with the self-legislated freedom, the past is erased (transposed on to Europe).[27]

In a similar fashion, the non-foundational 'epistemology' of postliberal theology does not rely on the often tradition-absent amnesia of modernity. In this manner, postliberal theology is intellectually postmodern, in that it denies the modern presup-position of possible epistemological neutrality. Instead, postliberal theology works within, speaks from, and embraces specific religious commitment.[28] The focus of postliberal theology is on the human individual within a particular ecclesial Christian context rather than on a grand scheme that justifies or explains overarching religious systems of thought. It does not deny truth, but it places the locus of truth within the context of the Christian community instead of imposing an outside notion of justifiable truth upon the community. As Thomas Guarino astutely clarifies:

> Postliberal thinkers argue, rather, that if one gives proper weight to the finite, the particular, and the local, then one speaks not of universal experiences and standards, but of enveloping cultural-linguistic systems, of encircling networks and webs of belief, of the incommensurability informing various conceptual

frameworks. Human thinking, acting, and judging are deeply rooted in the forms of life from which they emerge. And Christianity is not exempt from this determinacy. It too has its own forms of rationality and justification; its truth-warrants and criteria are to be found in the Christian community itself, not in universal standards imported or imposed from elsewhere.[29]

Aims of the book

Postliberal theology provides both an ecumenically constructive and corrective role to modernism, theological liberalism and conservative fundamentalism by attempting to renew and recapture the story of the Christian church by removing barriers that have contributed to its fragmentation whether in Europe or North America. It seeks to play restorative role to this divided, fractured church. This constructive and reparative role of postliberal theology to provide healing in and to the church is often ill considered by its critics.[30] The goal is more than lip service ecumenism, but rather aims for a unity of the Christian church catholic without compromising her diversity of expressions and backgrounds.

In view of this reparative role that postliberal theology seeks to play for the life and vitality of the church, it is worthy of thoughtful consideration by both theologians and parishioners in our postmodern climate. With this in mind, this book will attempt to provide an academic yet basic and accessible overview of the origins, key figures, current thought, potential problems and future possibilities for postliberal theology. This first chapter has attempted to provide some introductory descriptions, themes and purposes of postliberal theology to set the stage for these further observations.

Chapter 2 will highlight various background disciplines and selected influential scholars that have shaped the thought and central themes of postliberal theology. In the first portion of the second chapter, we will consider philosophical influences most notably seen in the work of Ludwig Wittgenstein and Alasdair McIntyre, along with the philosopher of science, Thomas Kuhn. This will be followed by mentioning insights of the noted cultural anthropologist, Clifford Geertz, as well as the sociological work of Peter Berger and Thomas Luckmann.

In the second portion of the second chapter, as we mentioned earlier, we call attention to three primary theologians whose work has shaped the development of the primary emphases in postliberal theology. We will mention two church fathers: St Augustine and Thomas Aquinas. Then we will focus on the work of one of the most preeminent modern church theologians, Karl Barth, who is arguably the most significant theological influence on the origins and development of postliberal theology.

In Chapter 3, we will consider several of the most influential theological exponents of postliberal theology. First, we will briefly discuss the noted Yale theologians Hans Frei and George Lindbeck. This will be followed by a discussion of the esteemed American theologian, Stanley Hauerwas. Finally, we will mention postliberal theological themes noticed in other theological voices such as David Kelsey, William Placher, Bruce Marshall, George Hunsinger, Kathryn Tanner and others. The purpose of this chapter is to provide a broad-stroke overview of major voices behind postliberal theology while at the same time mentioning other important contributions to the movement's development. Some theologians will be noticeably excluded due to the scope and purpose of this book, but we trust the authors we have chosen will provide the reader with the most salient features of this diverse theological expression. Many accounts of postliberal theology would properly include the work of Jewish theologian, Peter Ochs.[31] As C. C. Pecknold argues, Ochs provides a 'Jewish dialogical response to George Lindbeck' through his reading of Charles Sanders Pierce, to provide a 'shared scriptural pragmatism between Jews and Christians;' an important theme for Lindbeck. As with Lindbeck and other postliberal theologians, Ochs also is suggesting an alternative to the bankruptcy of modernist reasoning without becoming anti-modern.[32] Although we agree that Ochs' influence on the broader scholarship of this movement is arguably significant, we have chosen not to include his work in the discussion due to limitations of space and our primary focus on postliberal theology in the context of the particularity of the Christian narrative.

Chapter 4 will reflect on various problems and criticisms of postliberal theology. This will include the question of truth and falsity of beliefs, the problem of apologetics, the incommensurability between belief systems, religious diversity and the challenge of relating to culture and the public sphere. If the reality of Christian faith only surfaces in the context of the community, how then can we speak of truth? Further, what relationship does our particular faith context have with other expressions of faith? Can we defend our faith in response to other religious or nonreligious perspectives? Should we continue to advocate cross-denominational and cross-religious dialogue? This chapter will consider these questions along with possible responses from those advocating a postliberal perspective.

While keeping the problems and criticisms addressed in Chapter 4 in perspective, Chapter 5 will look to several ongoing prospects and proposals for continuing, modifying, and supplementing a robust postliberal Christian theology for today. We will support the postliberal repudiation of rationalism and consider how a chastened view of rationality, coupled with a recovery of intellectual humility, can help point the way forward in doing theology with postliberal sensitivities. Additionally, we will consider how our affections relate to our liturgical practices in the Christian community, along with the role of the Holy Spirit. We will finish by considering other prospects for guarding and continuing the heart of the postliberal theological vision.

The conclusion of the book will provide a brief summary with closing reflections on our investigations. We have also provided a guide for further reading at the back of this book, at the end of the conclusion. We fully understand that doing an introductory book of this nature requires mining the resources of other diligent scholars who have previously 'paved the way' by completing extensive critical research on this movement. The guide for further reading includes those authors of whom we are greatly indebted for guiding and instructing us in this more generalized research.

There are both strengths and weaknesses to the approach adopted in this book. We have attempted to concentrate on several major themes that characterize a loosely defined movement that has been addressed as 'postliberal theology'.[33] By considering the various general strands of criticisms of postliberal theology and identifying those strands within the context of the authors we have identified in Chapter 3, we will stay firmly committed to the purpose and intent of this book. The weakness of this approach is the tendency to oversimplify and neglect the nuances of particular authors that are already subsumed under the category of 'postliberal theologians' prior to their particular evaluation.

Certainly, superficiality or exaggeration is not the intention of this book, even though we are focusing on general themes and common threads. It is our desire to be fair to the particular authors considered while at the same time illustrating how their work has contributed to a movement with some common features and common problems.

CHAPTER 2

Background

Philosophical/anthropological/ sociological background

Any named system of thought, theological development or critical challenge for a change of perspective is indebted to other thinkers who have paved the way and opened the doors for renewed reflective practices. Postliberal theology is no exception. In fact, postliberal theology draws on several significant disciplines that include philosophy, ethics, philosophy of science, anthropology and sociology. Although we will make some noticeable omissions due to the requirements of space and focus of this book, we will briefly sketch three primary philosophical influences behind postliberal thinking. First, we will consider the philosopher Ludwig Wittgenstein, followed by an excursus on the theologian Paul Holmer, who is often credited with introducing Wittgenstein's philosophy to the theological world. Next, we will look at the ethical philosopher Alasdair MacIntyre, continued by noting the insights of the philosopher of science, Thomas Kuhn.

Following these philosophical influences, we will briefly consider the respected cultural anthropologist, Clifford Geertz, along with the reputable work of sociologists Peter Berger and Thomas Luckmann. Although we will not immediately make all the connections between these thinkers and postliberal theology in these brief synopses, the links to these thinkers will become extremely clear as we consider the primary exponents of postliberal theology in

Chapter 2. It is not our intent to demonstrate that these various thinkers are inextricably linked to each particular postliberal theologian mentioned, but rather to highlight how some basic ideas from these thinkers have profoundly influenced the writings and convictions of postliberal theologians in general.

Philosophy: Ludwig Wittgenstein (1889–1951)

Austrian-born Cambridge professor, Ludwig Wittgenstein, is one of the most influential philosophers of the twentieth century. Although baptized and buried as a Roman Catholic, he was not a practising man of faith throughout his lifetime. Nevertheless, Wittgenstein's philosophy seemed to be consistently haunted by religion, as his thoughts and themes have proved to have profound religious and theological implications. He is most known in theological circles for his notion of 'language games' introduced in his later work, *Philosophical Investigations*. His earlier work was more typical of analytic logical positivism, where language was said to picture reality. But his later writings unfolded a view of language that was more rich and expansive. Rather than language having a simple one-to-one correspondence to objects or reality, language is used in a variety of activities of human life and frameworks of meaning that include giving commands, reporting events, making jokes, telling stories and so forth. The meaning of language depends on how it is used in particular settings.[1] There are scientific as well as religious language games that are used within their own specific contexts. It is not right to impose scientific language games on religion, neither should religious scholars insist on their language games in scientific discussions. With some language games it is vitally important to consider the evidence for truth statements, with other language games it is not. Likewise, the type of certainty you may expect from a mathematical equation would look completely different from the kind of certainty you could expect in knowing whether your friend was truly in pain. It completely depends on the type of language game to which you would be referring. This concept of language games challenged the modernist understanding of universal objectivity along with its supporting historical foundations. Language is social and particular in its applicability, not universally experiential.[2] Wittgenstein effectively alerted us to respect the particularity of the usage of language in context.

For the later Wittgenstein then, language must be rescued from metaphysics and put into what he called 'everyday use'. Grammar works contextually, depending on how language is used; it is not universally based on some sort of metaphysical understanding of language. This emphasis on meaning as related to 'use' is central to understanding Wittgenstein's language games, and as we will see, becomes a key component when it is applied to postliberal theology. Words have meaning within a context of that which is teachable and learnable in ordinary language. If they are not, they have moved into the realm of what Wittgenstein called 'private language'. For example, we cannot point to an object while turning to a child and tell her it is 'probably' a chair, without first assuming this child knows what a chair is. It is important to know what a chair is in the context of ordinary, teachable language. This does not exempt the technical language of a specialist in any given field, for even technical vocabulary can be ordinary language, according to Wittgenstein, as long as it 'in principle' may be taught to others. If we allow philosophy to go beyond the limits of teachability in the ordinary language games of everyday use, then it will only cause confusion not be doing the work that it should in connecting meaning with teaching.[3]

As mentioned before, language has a variety of functions from making demands or promises, expressing hope, recounting events and asking questions; so the meaning of language completely depends on how it is used in its particular context. My students from the Netherlands or Ukraine would be confused if I told them a tall story and followed my words by the statement, 'I am only pulling your leg.' When they looked down and realized that their legs were indeed perfectly intact, they would be assured of my lunacy. It would be up to me to describe how I intended these words to be used in a particular context; the dictionary itself would be of little help. Wittgenstein's use of 'language games' helps to make precisely this point. If we impose one particular set of rules on language without considering its various forms of usage and context, then we make serious mistakes. It makes no sense for the biologist to impose her rules of empirical investigation on the poet or the theologian, and vice versa.[4]

Wittgenstein speaks to this problem clearly in his 'Lectures on Religious Belief'. In religious discourse, those that affirm such things as the Resurrection and the Last Judgement would not speak of their beliefs in terms of opinion, hypothesis, probability or even knowledge. Instead, words such as 'dogma', 'faith' and 'belief' are used in this context. The way in which one uses vocabulary when speaking to religious matters is different from the way it is used in scientific discourse. Some claim that Christianity is, without a doubt, historically based. Wittgenstein submits, however, that Christianity does not rest on history in the same sense as other historic facts. In this regard, ordinary historic facts cannot be considered foundational for religious beliefs. Those who have faith do not apply doubt in the same manner in which doubt could be applied to other historical propositions.[5]

But it is not that beliefs are *un*reasonable for Wittgenstein, but they are not reason*able*. Since the word 'unreasonable' is taken as a reproof on faulty human judgement, it gives the wrong impression of what he was trying to say. Perhaps it is better said that religious beliefs are not trying to fit in with the paradigm that we know as 'reasonability'. Again, it is not that the beliefs themselves are wrong, but when beliefs are made to conform with a system of reason that is foreign to the nature of those beliefs, then reason is wrongly applied; reason is not used or applied in some contexts of belief. In doing this, Wittgenstein effectively challenges us to think about the limits of philosophical and/or metaphysical discourse. It is not that Wittgenstein is assuming that one must abandon theological or philosophical discourse, but that when it is done, it need not be in conformity with some modernist notions of epistemic acceptability or face rejection.[6] In other words, modernist ideals do not set the standards for theology.

Jeannine Fletcher provides an example of how the idea of language games may also be applied within religious discourse itself. She suggests that the term 'Christ' has various meanings depending on its context. It may refer to the prophesied 'Messiah', the historical person of Jesus, the character of Jesus in the gospel narratives, a spiritual reality or even used as a curse word when one's fist slams on the table. The meaning of the word 'Christ' changes depending on its particular context and its following practice.[7] Although we may be reluctant to acknowledge the distinctive language game differences between the historical Jesus, Jesus as Messiah and Christ as a 'spiritual reality' to the degree that Fletcher seems to do, her application of Wittgenstein's language games challenges us to remember that religious words and their meanings are related to particular contexts of understanding within which the words are communicated and applied.

Excursus on Paul Holmer: Wittgenstein in dialogue with theology

Paul Holmer was a colleague of both Hans Frei and George Lindbeck at Yale. He is not one of the most well-known figures associated with postliberal theology, but his book, *The Grammar of Faith* (1978), is duly significant for its groundwork of implicitly integrating Wittgenstein's philosophy with theology. At the very least, Holmer should be considered a 'forerunner of postliberal theology'.[8] We will take this opportunity to provide an excursus on Holmer *as* a precursor to postliberal theology, and illustrate how he draws on Wittgenstein, albeit not uncritically, as a conversation partner in his book.

Holmer forthrightly states: 'theology is interpretation.' By this he does not mean that theology is reduced to relativism, but he is pointing out that there is no such thing as an 'utterly disengaged', unbiased neutrality when speaking of any sort of 'facts'. Neither is it the case that scientific or historical analyses are about stating objective facts, whereas theology is reduced to subjective interpretations. This is simply wrongheaded. Instead, Holmer submits that there are a variety of ways by which we gain understandings into various disciplines of thought. Also, there are different ways by which we attribute and apply the concept of 'fact' depending on the context.[9]

Holmer appears to indirectly refer (at the very least) to Wittgenstein when he claims that whether we are speaking of historical studies or theology that both are like games, in that within each discipline 'we can play the field according to the rules. But there is no subgame basic to all the rest.'[10] The manner of interpretation is different between the disciplines. One is theological, referring to God and godliness; the other is historical, concerned with past and present, causes and consequences. Holmer contends that the latter 'game' (the historical) is the newer one, only realized within recent 'history' and revealed in a markedly public manner. But neither reveals *the* one and only understanding or reality.

There are different sorts of facts that include historical facts and theological facts. We need both. The theology 'game' is one we must play when we speak to our lives as Christians following God. It is not the case that everything theological demands historical understanding, as if historical understanding were the basic 'game' governing all the others. Christian theology is not simply an intellectual system in line with modern understandings of that which is deemed reasonable by the masses, but it is rather shaped by God working in the human heart.[11]

Following his introductory chapter in *The Grammar of Faith*, Holmer describes the meaning of his title drawing on Wittgenstein: 'There is merit to the notion projected by Ludwig Wittgenstein that theology is the grammar of faith.'[12] Just as grammar provides the rules for communication in language, and those rules become absorbed, assumed and practiced by its users (even if not perfectly), so theology provides the grammar for carrying out the practice of Christianity. Holmer draws on Wittgenstein's notion of theology as grammar to provide a logical structure by which the Christian faith functions.[13] D. Stephen Long elucidates Holmer's adaptation of Wittgenstein when he speaks to this logic of grammar with regard to faith:

> If we know how to worship the Triune God, if we know how to go on in a consistent way, then of course we have a logical community across time and space as to who God is. Otherwise we would simply have a series of disconnected fragments. ... How we must live in this world shows consistent logics in our languages and practices, even if they are never completely translatable. The logic that lets us know how to go on prevents Christianity from being pure construction, non-sense, or just free play. It allows for Christianity to have both its own logic and at the same time a logic that anyone who uses language could understand.[14]

Despite noting Holmer's merits in accord with Wittgenstein, Long believes that Holmer takes Wittgenstein's critique of the metaphysical use of language as a critique of metaphysics itself. Long astutely point out that Wittgenstein did not suggest the abandonment of metaphysics *in toto*, but seems rather to be critiquing a version of metaphysics that supposes that we can use language to describe that which is beyond the language of everyday use. In other words, it is mistaken to think that we can use language to communicate something that may in fact not be possible to communicate using language. Instead, Long submits that we should understand that the grammar of language depends on truth, that is, truth makes language possible.[15] In view of this, Long make the following parallel to theology:

> Theology is similar to metaphysics. That should not be denied. If, as Holmer and the theological tradition have always argued, God is not an object in the world, then the concept 'God' requires 'metaphysics,' and theologians should not shy away from it. But a metaphysical *use* of language claims to give the human subject a reference point outside of language that sets limits to what language can do.[16]

One may certainly criticize, as Wittgenstein did, a certain version of metaphysics without denying another. For example, the French Roman Catholic philosopher, Jean-Luc Marion, provides a harsh critique on metaphysics as onto-theo-logy. By this Marion means that God is often forced into our modernist model of metaphysics that requires God to enter our conversation on the terms set by a Hellenistic model of 'Being'. This is no way implies that Marion is denying the reality of God. In fact, it is just the opposite. He is, in fact, affirming the God of scripture, the God who is beyond our own presumptive arrogant discourse and false images we have made of God.[17] The denial of this brand of metaphysics helpfully supplements the key points we wish to draw out from Wittgenstein and Holmer (and Wittgenstein via Holmer) as we note their impact on the development of postliberal theological expression. As we have noted, a primary impetus behind the moves of postliberal theology is to go beyond liberal theology's agenda that adapts and complies with the terms set by modernist rationalism and empiricism. For the postliberal theologian, theology's job is not to fit in with modernism, but to understand God and make Him known in the context of community practice in spite of our intellectual limitations.[18] The outside world must fit in with scripture's testimony and story of reality, rather than scripture's testimony continually seeking readjustment with the changing stories of the secularized world around us that wrongly exalts the hard sciences as the only means to truth and reality.

Hence, Paul Holmer demonstrates his precursory role to postliberal theology by emphasizing that theological inquiry cannot be equated to the same kind of scientific inquiry that is made with physics or geology. It is not that one form of understanding is to be favoured over the other; in fact, it is exactly this kind of polemicizing that Holmer rejects. Of course, he is primarily refuting the perpetuation of the belief that scientific inquiry has more clout to set the terms for what is deemed rational than religion, since religion is relegated to the irrational. For Holmer, both the languages of science and religion have aspects of rationality, since rationality is a concept that is 'polymorphic', depending on the topic and particular interests involved. Additionally, Holmer seems to be saying that if theology is made primarily into a mode of academic pursuit as other sciences, with an overemphasized stress on doctrinal propositions and systematic inquiry, then the nature of our Christian faith is skewed and reduced to intellectual understanding.[19]

This is where Holmer's challenge, and the challenge of postliberal theology in general, is a call to return to humility in our religious understandings. It is a call to reform our too often emphasized modernist, rational apologetic approaches to the Christian faith. If we desire evidences of the sort that are reserved for scientific inquiry, then our commitment to our religious faith will always seem premature. But this does not mean that religious faith is irrational or ridiculous simply because it requires a different sort of understanding prior to belief than is demanded from the hard sciences. The manner by which we come to understand the Christian faith is within a community context where we read, see, experience, commit and practise our faith (not necessarily in this order!). Too often we have allowed outside sources steeped in positivism to set the agenda for our faith commitments, assuming that the outside sources have the means by which to judge and evaluate all claims to facts, truth and understanding. Instead, if we realize that all forms of understanding have limits, methods and various contexts for communication and proclamation of what is 'real', then we realize that religious faith need not be dependent on such outside sources for verification, justification or viability. But we must postpone the development of these thoughts to a later chapter.

In order to gain 'knowledge' of God, we do not stack up empirical evidences. Moreover, we do not come to know God by simply using the word 'God' in certain religious contexts. As Holmer states: 'The true God is known only when his identity is established in a tradition and by a ruled practice of language and worship. This is what the grammar, the theology, provides.'[20] To truly know God means we must be committed to God Himself; we must become godly individuals, humbled before Him, realizing His caring, faithful presence in our lives.[21] This is the kind of 'knowledge' that is simply beyond the knowledge that is derived from a sterile laboratory. Instead it proceeds from a love that 'surpasses' knowledge (Eph. 3.19). This Wittgensteinian reworking of knowledge according to tradition and love in the practices of Christian community becomes extremely instructive for postliberal theology.

Moral philosophy: Alasdair MacIntyre (1929–)

Similar to what Wittgenstein does with language and words, Alasdair MacIntyre applies to ethics. MacIntrye, a well-known British moral philosopher, is professor emeritus and the Rev. John A. O'Brien Senior Research Professor of Philosophy at the University of Notre Dame. He is highly critical of Enlightenment and Anglo-American analytic philosophy that has entirely lost the ethical premodern vision. He denounces a grand universal scheme set up by a modernist agenda, for ethical absolutes. MacIntyre equally disdains the widely accepted claims of emotivism that abandon absolutes, which has also become a part of our culture. Emotivism understands moral judgements as simply expressions of personal preferences or moral feelings; hence, moral differences cannot be settled in a rational manner. Instead, MacIntyre argues that ethics must be applied contextually, considering the virtues within our particular communities and inherited traditions.[22] MacIntyre puts it this way: 'There is no standing ground, no place for enquiry, no way to engage in the practices of advancing, evaluating, accepting, and rejecting reasoned argument apart from that which is provided by some particular tradition or other.'[23] The idea of attaining a neutral position by which one may appraise traditions outside of one's own, or some universal rational understanding that is completely independent of tradition, is merely an illusion. The standards for that which is considered rational are only accessible within a given tradition. But MacIntyre's insistence on the socially embedded nature of our ethics does not disqualify claims of truth, but it rather submits that truth is always contextual.[24] He is not advocating ethical relativism, neither is he placing moral judgements into the hands of individual preferences, but he insists that our ethical decisions are always situated in the contexts of our particular traditions.

MacIntyre uses the concept of 'goods' to illustrate his point about how virtues are embedded in human community. With modernity the production of goods moved outside the local household and put to the 'service of impersonal capital', away from their regenerating force within the community of human families in order to sustain the broader community. Goods became the private property of the egotist, rather than shared community resources. Within the household, there was place for everyone to contribute to the broader whole. Unmarried women were valuable as 'spinsters', the ones who would spin the wool. But they were valued members of the home. Unfortunately, at the dawn of modernism in the eighteenth century, the word 'spinster' took on derogatory connotations as community virtues were compromised for the sake of a more individualist culture.[25] MacIntyre affirms that a shared vision and understanding of goods is essential for laws and virtues:

> To cut oneself off from shared activity in which one has initially to learn obediently as an apprentice learns, to isolate oneself from the communities which find their point and purpose in such activities, will be to debar oneself from finding any good outside of oneself. It will be to condemn oneself to that moral solipsism which constitutes Nietzschean greatness.[26]

Indeed, virtues and virtuous living should not be separated from community engagement and practice; they are for the benefit and sustenance of that community within its tradition, not merely for the self-indulgent individual.

Hence, for MacIntyre, beliefs are expressed through rituals and practice in the context of community. The reformulation of beliefs is not some sort of intellectual activity typical of the 'Cartesian mind', but takes place through social individuals relating to each other. But lest we misunderstand, MacIntyre also submits that what is said within a particular tradition may 'be heard or overheard by those in another'. Out of respect, traditions may share certain perspectives or beliefs even though they may radically differ.[27] As Jeffrey C. K. Goh observes, '[MacIntyre] is acutely aware of what appears to follow from the claim that rationality is only internal to particular traditions.'[28] Goh points out that MacIntyre will not accept the Enlightenment-derived dilemma of needing to choose between the notion of a universally accessible rationality, on one hand, or relativism, on the other. Instead, rationality is seen as a 'tradition-constituted and tradition-constitutive enquiry'– a rationality that is both embedded in tradition, yet continues to develop through time. MacIntyre is not willing to throw the entire 'baby' of rationality out with the abuses of the modern rationalistic bathwater. He wants to affirm the possibility of ongoing dialogue between those of different traditions, while at the same time emphasizing the important role that tradition and context play in those traditions.[29] For MacIntyre, accepting tradition and the diversity that brings must not lead to the concession of relativism.

For MacIntrye this understanding of 'tradition-constituted' rationality may be the most disposed toward further enquiry and dialogue when it faces an 'epistemological crisis' that stems from internal inconsistencies within the tradition. If one is faced with possible differences of interpretation, a new narrative must emerge in order to explain the reasons behind the older beliefs along with the new. MacIntyre's notion of tradition supposes that conflict will remain both within and between various traditions. His perspective on tradition coupled with his progressive or transitional view of rationality allows for participants within traditions to continue to translate and retranslate their beliefs when faced with various challenges while at the same time maintaining belief essentials representing the heart of their particular traditions.[30] As MacIntyre puts it: 'A rational tradition's modes of continuity differ from those of the former, its ruptures from those of the latter. Some core of shared belief, constitutive of allegiance to the tradition, has to survive every rupture.'[31]

MacIntyre's proposal of a tradition-constituted rationality certainly will not meet the demands of onlookers insisting on objective truth. Nonetheless, MacIntyre may not be accused of discounting truth, for truth is still the goal of his tradition-centred mode of enquiry. Likewise, rationality is important and must not simply be jettisoned due to its improper excesses in modernity. But rationality is only accessible from within the context of our tradi-tions.[32] MacIntyre refuses to meet the demands of 'objective' truth because objectivity is often confused with neutrality, and neutrality and truth are by no means co-dependent. Access to truth is only made visible through the lens of tradition and community.

Philosophy of science: Thomas Kuhn (1922–96)

Thomas Kuhn was an extremely influential American philosopher of science, holding advanced degrees in physics. He taught at such notable institutions as Harvard, Berkeley, Princeton and the Massachusetts Institute of Technology. Kuhn's work revealed the 'scandal' of science. That which Wittgenstein addressed as 'language games' for various activities and disciplines of life, Kuhn applied to scientific discourse. Scientific inquiry in general is not a neutral enterprise for uncovering all truth. This becomes clear in what Kuhn called 'paradigm shifts' in science. In his ground-breaking book, *The Structure of Scientific Revolutions*, Kuhn proposed that not only is science itself a different language game from religion but also various language games are noticeable within scientific discourse itself. For example, for a chemist, the helium atom is considered a molecule because of activity with respect to the kinetic theory of gases. But, for the physicist, no molecular spectrum is displayed; so it is not considered a molecule. Both scientists are looking at the same particle from two different paradigms, depending on their particular field of research. Kuhn astutely shows how this type of incommensurability is seen throughout the history of science, the criteria for scientific evalu-ation change depending on one's particular paradigm or worldview that governs the particular field of investigation. Hence, paradigm shifts in science are due more to social factors rather than factors that pertain to the increase of factual knowledge.[33]

For Kuhn, scientific data are always mediated through and shaped by the categories of particular communities. We always see and understand the phenomenal world through the lens in which we are situated. Although our paradigms will in one sense restrict our extent of knowledge, since the focus will be inevitably be placed (even inadvertently) on the concerns of the community, they also provide the means by which scientific data may be organized.

It is not that Kuhn is mourning the absence of pure neutrality when doing science; instead, paradigms are the means by which we can do scientific investigation. Paradigms train our interpretations and perceptions through the practice of applying the paradigms within our various particular community contexts. Interpretations of data will end up being different, because the data themselves are shaped within the context of the paradigm. It is inevitable that paradigms will inevitably leave out some aspects by concentrating on others.[34] Nevertheless, in spite of this acknowledged partiality, paradigms still guide, govern and make possible scientific research.

Also, we may be able to identify a paradigm used in research even if we cannot identify all of its rules of use. Kuhn submits that the Hungarian philosopher of science, Michael Polanyi (1891–1976), went a similar direction through his theme of 'tacit knowledge', which is knowledge that is acquired through practice. Kuhn develops this idea by referring to Wittgenstein on this point. For Wittgenstein, we would not list all the rules of use for a word such as 'game' or 'chair' in order to understand the meaning of the word 'game' or 'chair'. Instead, we recognize the 'family resemblance' of these terms by its networking of resemblances in order to identify and provide the given term. Kuhn submits that this idea may be applied to the world of scientific inquiry as well. It is not that different research questions must satisfy a given set of explicitly common rules, but instead they relate by resemblance to another aspect of previously acknowledged understanding of achievement and models of inquiry within the scientific community at large.[35] Scientists and philosophers alike may not be able to cite and list all the rules of investigation that govern their respective disciplines, but this does not reduce their research to mere relativistic inquiry. Indeed their research is directed, but it is not governed by adherence to a specific set of rules, but by following accepted, practised norms of behaviour that have shaped and developed their disciplines for years. It is not that the disciplines are absent of any rules, but the 'rules', like paradigms, are more tacitly in place within the context of the particular research community's practices.

The implications for theological discourse (and more specifically for postliberal theology) as may be expected, are similar to Wittgenstein's language games:

> Thus, just as communities of scientists see the world in a particular way based on the paradigms they use, so too, religious

communities see the world in a particular way based on the sacred texts that function as paradigms for them. Believers see the world imaginatively through scriptural lenses, allowing the structure of their narratives themselves to organize the sensory stimuli of the world. Within the pages of the sacred text are found the categories that shape religious persons' experiences of the world.[36]

But seeing the world imaginatively through the lens of the narrative of scripture is not to be construed as anti-realist or reduced to a fairytale-like rendering of the world. Instead, the lens of scripture in practice by the community is the means of access to the world God has given.

Of course, there are limitations as to what extent Kuhn's work may be appropriated by postliberal theological perspectives. Robert Shedinger points out that for Kuhn, scientific progress is marked by an 'evolutionary enterprise' moving from paradigm to paradigm (always with a degree of resistance). With each new paradigm also comes a new emerging scientific community that shares the paradigm. As we have suggested, and we will continue to see, postliberal theology is concerned about 'paradigms' of religious communities and how they serve to root the theological and religious practices of those communities. This is not to say that these religious paradigmatic expressions of community faith are seeking to evolve in order to truly do what they are intended to do.[37] In fact, it is generally the opposite. Postliberal theology is doing more than merely providing a theological description of the way we go about believing what we believe, but it is also about our theological commitments to particular Christian communities and Christian practices within those communities.

Cultural anthropology: Clifford Geertz (1926–2006)

In addition to this philosophical background, postliberal theology also draws insights from American cultural anthropologist, Clifford Geertz. Geertz served in the US Navy during World War Two, studied philosophy as an undergraduate then went on to do doctoral work in anthropology at Harvard. Throughout his career he taught primarily as a professor at the University of Chicago and Princeton University.

Geertz borrows the notion of 'thick description', to describe his cultural anthropological work, from the philosopher Gilbert Ryle. By 'thick description', Geertz is referring to ethnographic description, a semiotic perspective of culture with humans in various webs of significance. Such ethnographic description examines the webs and flows of social discourse in order to gain some sort of conceptual insight into the subjects in question. The point of such ethnography is not to systematically harmonize all observed regularities in culture, but to make what is called a 'thick description' by providing generalizations within various cases of culture.[38] As Geertz writes:

> Rather than beginning with a set of observations and attempting to subsume them under a governing law, such inference begins with a set of (presumptive) signifiers and attempts to place them within an intelligible frame. Measures are matched to theoretical predictions, but symptoms (even when they are measured) are scanned for theoretical peculiarities—that is, they are diagnosed. In the study of culture the signifiers are not symptoms or clusters of symptoms, but symbolic acts or clusters of symbolic acts, and the aim is not therapy but the analysis of social discourse. ... In ethnography, the office of theory is to provide a vocabulary in which what symbolic action has to say about itself—that is, about the role of culture in human life—can be expressed.[39]

For Geertz, religion itself is a symbolic system of culture that is expressed through public transactions that are mediated symbolically, enforced by ritualistic practices and transform the world of its participants both individually and collectively. But there is an ongoing dialectic between religion as a symbolic system and the religious experiences of its followers. Religious culture affects experiences, but the experiences continue to change and develop the religious culture.[40] The beliefs of the symbolic system of religion, as with other symbolic systems, result in practices that both change and continue to govern the lives of the believers and continue to shape beliefs.

Geertz works this idea out in one of his classic essays titled, 'Religion as a Cultural System'. Geertz examines what it means to believe in a religious context. He refused to accept a Durkheimian influenced notion of forcing religion into science. Religious beliefs do not arise from 'Baconian induction' but rather from a 'prior acceptance of authority' that transforms our everyday experience. This would be true for Geertz whether we are speaking of Christianity or tribal or mystical religions. Regardless of these differences, the basic and common axiom behind 'the religious perspective' is that someone who claims to have knowledge must first believe.[41] And it is this 'belief' that stems from the prior commitment to the authority to which Geertz was referring.

Geertz introduces what he labels the 'religious perspective' by declaring that a 'perspective' is one particular mode or way of viewing reality among others. He postulates that the particular features of such religious perspective emerge if we compare it to other major 'perspectives' of seeing the world, such as the 'everyday' world of common sense, the scientific perspective and the aesthetic perspective. Common sense is derived from years of cultural shaping by generation after generation. 'Common sense' is the label given to those matters that are seen as obvious ways of interpreting and doing things that are common among those within a particular cultural context. Within a scientific framework of perception, however, this obvious given nature to the way things operate vanishes. Instead of making simple assumptions, science demands that its hypotheses be put through the rigours of doubt and careful systematic analysis. The aesthetic perspective, unlike the scientific perspective, does not radically question the things that appear to us in everyday life, but instead concentrates on how they appear to us in their shapes and forms and visible qualities.[42]

But the religious perspective, for Geertz, looks beyond everyday realities to the wider realities of teleology, and calls for faith in those realities. It does not put such realities to empirical testing as the scientific perspective would do, but it is rather questioned through the grid of an accepted 'wider' teleology. It focuses on commitment to belief, rather than scepticism of belief. Rather than reducing reality to the aesthetic or ignoring factuality, the religious perspective concentrates on ultimate reality and its symbolic expressions in ritual.[43] Geertz claims:

> [I]t is in ritual—that is, consecrated behavior—that the conviction that religious conceptions are veridical and that religious directives are sound is somehow generated. ... In a ritual, the world as lived and the world as imagined, fused under the agency of a single set of symbolic forms, turn out to be the same world.[44]

Does God fit into this picture at all? Geertz is not completely clear on this. But he does indicate that the framework of the scientist must not be imposed on religious expressions of faith. He claims that if 'divine intervention' has any role to play in all then 'it is not the business of the scientist to pronounce upon such matters one way or the other' because it is simply outside the boundaries of a scientific field of inquiry. Regardless of any supernatural intervention, at the human level Geertz insists that religious convictions definitely stem from specific and concrete religious practices.[45] As we will see, it is this of linking of convictions (and hence beliefs) to religious practices where we notice the deep reverberation of Geertz's thought in postliberal theology.

Geertz is not saying that having a religious perspective is mutually exclusive of other perspectives. If one holds a certain religious perspective, and lives in and through the reality of religious symbols, it does not mean that one lives like this every moment in life. In fact, most people would only live in such a 'reality' at particular moments or during certain events, whereas the commonsense perspective may regulate the greater portion of life's events.[46] As Geertz adds: 'A man, even large groups of men, may be aesthetically insensitive, religiously unconcerned, and unequipped to pursue formal scientific analysis, but he cannot be completely lacking in common sense and survive.'[47] But does one's religious perspective colour one's view of the common sense? Certainly it does, as Geertz agrees. This would vary, however, from religion to religion and the nature of the cosmic reality in which the one committed to a certain religion has come to embrace. Of course, this does not speak to the truth or falsity of religious claims themselves, or whether or not notions of religious experience are in fact authentic; but Geertz points out that such questions cannot be addressed from the sole vantage point of a scientific perspective.[48] He understands that authenticity depends on the particular claim within a particular context.

Although Geertz rarely cites Wittgenstein, Wittgenstein's later philosophical writings most obviously coloured Geertz's work in anthropology. For Geertz, culture of a people group is akin to a collection of texts, and within that people group or society, as with individual lives, are particular interpretations. Nevertheless, in spite of the obvious influences, it was not until a few decades after Geertz published *The Interpretation of Cultures* that he finally came to grips with how much he was impacted by Wittgenstein's notion of language games as a 'set of practices'. As Wittgenstein's language games illustrate that the meaning of terms is linked to context and practice, so Geertz demonstrates that the meaning of behaviours and statements only comes by a full understanding of 'the cultural context as a life-form'. So we not only need to understand particular language games of those with whom we dialogue, but we must also carefully consider their communal contexts.[49] Despite these different and nonetheless helpful emphases of Wittgenstein and Geertz, we believe it is also important to stress that language and culture within communal contexts cannot be divorced. Language is a part of culture, as culture is a part of language. They are inextricably connected and constantly overlapping. In fact, it is often impossible to make clear distinctions between the two. The words we use are used in a shared cultural context in order to function in a meaningful way within the community.

Sociology: Peter Berger (1929–) and Thomas Luckmann (1927–)

Peter Berger is a noted Austrian-born sociologist who has taught at Rutgers University, Boston College and is currently Professor Emeritus of Religion, Sociology and Theology at Boston University. Reminiscent of what we stressed with Clifford Geertz and culture, Berger likewise emphasizes that mankind shapes society and society shapes mankind. This is not contradictory, but rather reflects the dialectic and interdependence of the two. Berger expresses it this way in his book *The Sacred Canopy: Elements of a Sociological Theory of Religion*:

> Society is a dialectic phenomenon in that it is a human product, and nothing but a human product, that yet continuously acts back upon its producer. Society is a product of man. It has no other being that which is bestowed upon it by human activity and consciousness. There can be no social reality apart from man. Yet it may also be stated that man is a product of society. Every individual biography is an episode within the history of society, which both precedes and survives it. ... It is within

society, and as a result of social processes, that the individual becomes a person, that he attains and holds onto an identity, and that he carries out the various projects that constitute his life. Man cannot exist apart from society.[50]

Society is the internalized but 'objectivated' world of the individual. But the individual's biography is only objectively real as it is understood within the socially structured world.[51] So, for Berger, it is not that the individual is completely obliterated and replaced by society, but it is within the context of society where the individual person's meaning is made significant.

Thomas Luckmann, a German sociologist of Slovene origins, is a professor emeritus in sociology at the University of Konstanz, in Germany. Peter Berger and Thomas Luckmann co-authored a small but very influential book, *The Social Construction of Reality*. Berger and Luckmann argue for what the title declares: Reality is constructed by social determinants and the job of sociologists is to analyze how this occurs. By 'reality' Berger and Luckmann are certainly not denying the phenomena of the physical world, everyday objects such as toothbrushes, automobiles and chairs. Instead, they are linking words such as 'reality' and 'knowledge' in terms of their sociological understanding. The 'everyday' person takes for granted the 'everyday' things he or she takes to be real and assumes them to be items of knowledge. The *sociologist* looks at how these types of 'everyday' conception may vary from culture to culture, which is a different sort of analysis from that undertaken by the philosopher. For example, the meaning of 'reality' for a monk living in Tibet will be radically different than 'reality' for an American businessperson. As such, what passes for knowledge in each of these cultures will also be significantly different.[52] With this in mind Berger and Luckmann contend the following:

> [T]he sociology of knowledge must concern itself with whatever passes for 'knowledge' in a society, regardless of the ultimate validity or invalidity (by whatever criteria) of such 'knowledge.' And insofar as all human 'knowledge' is developed, transmitted and maintained in social situations, the sociology of knowledge must seek to understand the processes by which this is done in such a way that a taken-for-granted 'reality' congeals for the man in the street. In other words, we contend that *the sociology*

of knowledge is concerned with the analysis of the social construction of reality.[53]

Just as it may be argued that the agenda of postliberal theology is largely descriptive, describing the way that theology functions as the grammar of the church community, so Berger and Luckmann seek to maintain a non-polemical, descriptive tone to their sociological approach to human beings in relationship to the phenomenology of everyday social reality. Everyday life to the 'everyday' person appears 'objectified' prior to its appearance as 'reality'. Whatever is closest to people at a given time is experienced as 'real'. Yet, in this 'everydayness', it is understood that there are different 'zones' of 'closeness' and 'remoteness'. It is this sort of commonsense view of knowledge that is a sociological, shared understanding within one's social community that is assumed to be 'reality'; it is simply self-evident and obvious. For Berger and Luckmann, to stray from this commonsense understanding of knowledge and reality, one must intentionally deviate from the 'everyday' to the highly theoretical work of the philosopher.[54] The basic idea here is that the basis on which something is understood as reality in everyday life to the everyday person (whatever or whoever that may be!) is structurally different than the analytical work of a philosopher. It is not that the work of the philosopher or scientist is irrelevant, but their work is not necessarily contextually relevant to how we view reality from a sociological perspective.

In this age where scientific and philosophical epistemologies reign, Berger and Luckmann's sociological perspectives on knowledge provide a promising way forward. We often neglect to consider the sociological values, special interests and limitations behind our suppositions of knowledge that essentially constitute our perception of reality. At the same time, we must carry out an ongoing conversation between sociology, philosophy, history and science, understanding that there is no discipline that is inherently value free in its inquiry.[55] As we can see, this is a recurrent thread that runs through the various philosophers and thinkers we have examined: there is no neutral free zone in which we may enter to discover objective reality; it is always mediated by one's context and culture.

Our everyday life is characterized by primarily pragmatic concerns and efforts. For example, when someone uses the telephone, it is for a specific purpose and demands a pragmatic understanding of usage. We must understand how to dial and when to dial certain numbers based on long-distance requirements and time differences. We do not need to know all the technical details on why or how the telephone works, we simply need to know how to use the telephone to make our desired call. Of course, if the telephone fails to work, then we will be more interested than usual in its technical aspects, but otherwise we really do not care. We are saying all this to say that 'everyday knowledge' is knowledge of basic usage to accomplish practical agendas and there is usually no reason to move beyond this level of knowledge in our everydayness unless something breaks or interrupts the normal process of things. Our individual 'worlds' are basically structured and taken for granted according to very pragmatic routines, relative to individual lives, occupations and concerns.[56]

Others do share aspects of common knowledge with us. These are what Berger and Luckmann call 'relevance structures'. At times our relevance structures intersect with one another based on a common 'social stock' of knowledge. This helps us become aware of what and what not to speak to others. For example, we will not tell our doctor about our investment problems and our lawyer will not hear about our stomach pain. There is a 'social distribution of knowledge' that is shared differently by different sorts of people. I cannot know everything on every subject in order to navigate my daily life.[57] Knowledge is shared throughout the community and distributed based on perceived need. Knowledge must, in fact, be specialized knowledge to live in the specialized world of goods and services in which we live. If we were required to understand all of what we do in life through the grid of a highly complex epistemology, we would not be able to function at all.

Postliberal theology adapts and applies a major point from Berger and Luckmann: everyday life is about embodiment within institutionalized routines, with consistent reaffirmation in social interactions. In this regard, one's subjective reality stands in a relationship with a socially defined objective reality.[58] Berger and Luckmann themselves apply this to religion when they submit: 'Religion requires a religious community, and to live in a religious world requires affiliation with that community.'[59] Granted, we have not addressed how Berger and Luckmann explain divergences and abnormalities with those who do not integrate into the socialization process, neither have we discussed the nuances of their work as they differentiate between primary and secondary socialization. We will need to leave these aspects of their work with the reader for further investigation.[60] Nonetheless, we trust these insights have demonstrated, albeit briefly, the sociological implications of how we render the concepts of reality and knowledge in our everyday life and practices – including of course, our religious practices.

Although postliberal theology is known for its commitment and emphasis on the biblical text and narrative, its theological shape and development has certainly drawn on many 'outside' sources for its inspiration to keep 'inside' the faith narrative without demanding insularism. We have by no means exhausted the list of those who have exercised influence on postliberal theology and its theologians; if space permitted, there are arguably many more that could be added. Nonetheless, we trust that in this brief sketch some of the significant philosophical, anthropological, and sociological background sources of postliberal theology will help us understand the richness and variety of disciplines from which this movement draws its inspiration. We trust these influences will become even clearer as we discuss the formation of postliberal theology through several of its pivotal theological exponents. Before we do this, however, it will be helpful to take a look at three key theological background figures who have also left their indelible mark on the development of postliberal theology.

Theological background: St Augustine, Thomas Aquinas and Karl Barth

Whenever decisions are made about theologians who are considered the most influential on a certain period or system of thought within theology, certain oversights and generalizations are bound to occur. Notwithstanding, we believe at least three important theologians must be mentioned and briefly considered with respect to the historical theological formation of postliberal theology. Although Augustine and Aquinas are centuries apart from each other, both of them are also centuries apart from any theological movement that would be considered 'postliberal'. It is not our intent to suggest that these well-known fathers of the church are directly linked to postliberal theology, but their influence on the postliberal theological project is significant for understanding its development. We will limit ourselves to some simple observations and comments first on Augustine, then Aquinas. We will follow this by addressing the most significant theological influence on postliberal theology: Karl Barth.

St Augustine (354–430)

C.C. Pecknold argues that Aquinas was certainly an Augustinian, and it is Aquinas who is more explicitly referenced in postliberal theology, but the resources of Augustine himself should also be duly considered for understanding the background to this movement.[61] When George Lindbeck speaks to the postliberal theme of the 'scriptural world' absorbing the universe and supplying the framework of interpretation for understanding reality, he refers to Augustine: 'Augustine did not describe his work in the categories we are employing, but the whole of his theological production can be understood as a progressive, even if not always successful, struggle to insert everything from Platonism and the Pelagian problem to the fall of Rome into the world of the Bible.'[62]

Pecknold points out that for Augustine, as is seen later in George Lindbeck, scripture is a semiotic system for its participants in community. Augustine linked *signum* with the *sacramentum*, which affirmed that 'the sign' mysteriously revealed transcendent meaning. More specifically, the incarnation is the Word becoming flesh, and the scriptures, in form and content, also mediate the incarnate Word. Signs became sacramental for Augustine because they were used by God to mediate transcendent Truth. It is this mediation of the Word of God that makes the scriptures understandable to human beings as Scripture. This does not mean that textual mediation bridges the gap entirely; the community of faithful interpreters must work in community, fully engaged in hermeneutical participation to heal the 'semiotic ruptures'. Pecknold contends that Augustine believed that scripture itself teaches that we are to 'reason in community for the sake of the world' (Isaiah 1.16–18). The narrative of scripture is a world of its own, requiring its own epistemological privileges within the faith community. The Word was made flesh and now dwells within us; now we continue to live within the scriptures and put them into practice.[63] In this sense, the members of the community of faith become the living texts of the Word used by God for its ongoing mediation and performance.

Pecknold draws on the work of R. A. Markus in describing Augustine's 'triadicity of semiotics' to elucidate this mediation of the Word of God:

> [T]he meaningfulness of the sign is received within human community, and that such a community of sign-users will inevitably extend the meaningfulness of signs by discovering new relationships of signification. Why? For Augustine, it is because of this link between the Word and human language, between the divine self-giving of God in the Word made flesh and the ongoing communication of this God in scriptural signification.[64]

This process of communication in 'scriptural signification' is carried out by the faithful community in whom the scriptures are entrusted for performing the Word of God as the body of Christ. The faithful readers and interpreters of scripture become a 'textual replication, a living salvific text made flesh for the healing of the nations'.[65] It is this embodied Word, through the Holy Spirit, in the faith community, that continues to perform this word and mediate its gospel message to the world. In this regard, we can readily see how Pecknold is persuaded by the value of Augustine in both the influence on and ongoing consideration of postliberal theological themes.

Thomas Aquinas (1225–74)

Thomas Aquinas is touted by postliberal theologian, George Lindbeck, as one who put the foot of faith forward first, prior to any foundational arguments for that faith. Reason follows faith; it does not precede it. Lindbeck applies this to his postliberal theological paradigm when he says the that 'the logic of coming to believe, because it is like that of learning a language, has little room for argument, but once one has learned to speak the language of faith, argument becomes possible.'[66] William

Placher also accepts Aquinas' assertion that one may not have knowledge of things independently of the knowledge of the fact that God created them. In other words, it is God's creation that makes knowledge of theology possible since creation provides an analogical relation and participation between God and His creatures. Hence, knowledge of religion will not come through mere propositions, but through the narrative of the gospel as it is embodied and practised within the faith community. This knowledge will be formed inwardly by tradition according to what the Apostle Paul calls the 'mind of Christ' (1 Cor. 2.16) and to which Aquinas refers as 'connatural knowledge'. This connatural knowledge of practicing the faith comes via wisdom, discernment, and charity mediated by the Holy Spirit.[67] It is both Aquinas' nonfoundationalism along with his promotion of a 'connatural' participatory type of epistemology that is critically appropriated in postliberal theology.

Karl Barth (1886–1968)

Perhaps the major theological impetus behind postliberal theology is found in Karl Barth, who is arguably the most influential theologian of the twentieth century. Barth was born in Basel in 1886, to devoutly pietistic Christian parents. Barth's father was trained in theology and taught at the University of Bern. Karl Barth himself began university studies at Bern, continuing on to Berlin, Tübingen and finally at Marburg. Barth was immersed into the world of Protestant theological liberalism, especially under the influence of Wilhelm Herrmann. But Barth refused to let theological liberalism set the agenda for his theological understanding; neither was he wooed by the wooden literalism of fundamentalism. As we will see, Barth argued for a third way to revive theology from the snares and possession of modern culture.[68] In order to understand the shaping of Barth's thinking along these lines, it is essential to recall his personal context. It is well known that in the outbreak of the Great War (World War One) Barth's former theological mentors (including Wilhelm Hermann and Adolf von Harnack) signed support for Kaiser Wilhelm II's war policy. This was devastating for Barth. He saw it as a complete ethical failure not only of his professors, but also of the entire liberal theological enterprise.[69]

The absolutism of reason exalted the efforts of man over God and ironically ended up providing a theological justification for robbing humankind of its own dignity through German National Socialism.

While Barth was a pastor in Safenwil, Switzerland, he was working on a theological commentary on the book of Romans. In the course of his research he found, under the influence of Søren Kierkegaard, the God who is Wholly Other. God is beyond any natural theology or modern renditions of reasonability, He is completely beyond our rational understandings and judgements or anything that can be posed by a supposed natural theology. God is, as Barth echoed the words of Kierkegaard, the 'infinite qualitative distinction'.[70] Barth countered Enlightenment intellectual ideals that affirmed the self-made autonomous individual and the endless questioning of all prescientific notions of truth. The Enlightenment project, for Barth, simply opened the door for a natural theology to wrongly be the judge over the truth of 'revealed' theology. Instead, Barth claimed that theology is a '*free* science' – it 'respects the mystery of the freedom of its object' (God), and it is free from reliance upon external presuppositions to which it is subordinate.[71] Barth made this clearly evident through his composition of the Barmen Declaration of 1934, during the rise of Hitler and the Nazi Party. Barth, representing the Confessing Church of Germany, rejected the political tyranny of the National Socialists and refused to show compliance to Hitler. God is not subject to the state. God was certainly opposed to the Third Reich; therefore Barth was certainly opposed to the German state. As a result, he was forced to resign his post at the University of Bonn, and return to Switzerland where he took a faculty position at the University of Basel.

Although Barth was trained and deeply impacted personally by liberal theologians and their work, he ultimately saw such perspectives as conceding faith to modernity and historical positivism. Friedrich Schleiermacher's work laid the foundation for liberal theology that dominated nineteenth- and twentieth-century theology. Barth fully agreed with Schleiermacher's understanding of the radical importance of religion for helping us understand our lives. However, instead of allowing the broad category of religion to set the terms for understanding Christianity, Barth believed that religion must be understood from the particular grid of Christianity. We must look to Christ first and foremost to understand our human nature, not vice versa. Our Christian faith should not in any way be subjected to the warrants of modern rationality.[72] After all, why should modern intellectual standards set the terms for our faith? Faith has its own self-consistency; it is not dependent on some external superintendence. Robert Jenson provides this helpful insight regarding Barth in this regard:

> The assertions of faith, he argued, have their own internal coherence with one another, and demonstration of theology's rationality consists in tracing the spiderweb of their connections. Nor is this the coherence of an arbitrarily invented system, since the whole world which thus obtains is a single witness to an event outside itself, the event of Christ. Moreover, such knowledge, if it is knowledge at all, must be the decisive knowledge also about the world, for if faith is true then all things find their truth in Christ.[73]

Faith in Christ is not a privatized faith with no bearing on reality, but faith in Christ truly is reality.

For Barth, God cannot be conceived or known as just an object among other objects. If so, God is not God. 'Faith' knowledge is distinct and unique from all other sorts of knowledge. What this means specifically cannot be derived from the conception of humans, but only from God himself.[74] As Barth puts it: 'Since the One who unveils Himself is the God who by nature cannot be unveiled to men, self-unveiling means that God does what men themselves cannot do in any sense or in any way: He makes Himself present, known and significant to them as God.'[75] God's *knowability* is only made possible through His own triune nature and by His grace in Jesus Christ. God is completely sovereign over His *knowability*. For Barth, there is no absolute that is independent of or deeper than God's revelation of which God confers and God makes his word known. Human beings cannot in any way reach God through their own epistemological efforts.[76]

With this in mind, Barth did not see his job to make the Christian faith in some way valid or credible to the modern world. Instead, it is the world that must be made credible to Christianity. History must not be examined through the grid of Copernicus or Constantine, but through the life, death, resurrection and ascension of Jesus of Nazareth. So it is not a matter of translating Jesus into modern understandings, but of translating modernity to

Jesus.[77] Barth rejected any appeal to natural theology or necessary pre-understandings in order to get to faith. There is no possibility of a neutral appeal to logic, philosophy, or anthropology to set the terms or lay the foundations for Christianity.

Postliberal theology obviously inherited Barth's disdain of allowing non-Christian philosophical foundations dictate the context whereby the claims of Christianity must be justified. Instead, it is scripture and the narrative of Christianity itself that sets the framework for its own understanding. For Barth, it is wrongheaded to seek cognitive justification for Kingdom discourse in the discourse of the world apart from the Kingdom. It must be the other way around. Faith has its own internal coherence, structure for viability and internal rationality.[78]

When the narrative of God's word is revealed, this does not necessarily imply that one must historically defend that narrative. Of course, the narrative may have historical components, but this is not the point for Barth. The historical elements of scripture are part of a larger set of narrative genres that God uses to communicate. If we stress the apologetic defence of scripture's historicity, then we are placing ourselves in control of scripture. But scripture is not as much something we are called to master, as it is something that should master us.[79] If God is the 'infinite qualitative distinction,' the Wholly Other, Almighty, Creator of all, then does it not make sense that He sets the agenda on how we understand His word? It must be by His initiative entirely. If we seek understanding of God from natural theology and historical proofs they will always be tainted by our own self-preoccupied motives. But if God sets the agenda and He is the giver of revelation apart from any efforts of flawed human cognitive skill, then it is fruitless to look toward a modernist epistemology to justify our faith and the narrative of scripture.

With these things in mind, we will see where Hans Frei appropriated Barth's emphasis on theology proceeding by narrative and description, rather than by arguments or logical foundations. The Christian world consists of its own linguistic integrity and finds consistency within itself, similar to how a literary work of art is self-consistent within its own genre. It is not dependent on some pre-linguistic common understanding of reality. But, the Christian world is not directly equated with other worlds depicted in literature, because the world in which the Christian lives is the one common world for all living beings – the world in which we are all responsible.[80] We will see more of the unfolding of Barth's influence on Frei more specifically in the beginning of the following chapter as we consider the primary or seminal theological exponents of what is known as postliberal theology.

CHAPTER 3

Theological exponents of postliberal theology

We will divide this chapter into three major sections, which are somewhat artificial distinctions. The first section traces the beginning of what is commonly called, the 'Yale School', with (in our estimation) the two most primary representatives and pioneers of postliberal theology, Hans Frei and George Lindbeck. There are certainly others who should be rightfully be considered under the Yale School, such as David Kelsey, but we are limiting ourselves in this section to postliberal theology's most influential contributors and major exponents, therefore we are including Kelsey under a later section. In the second section, we will consider the community-centred ethic of Stanley Hauerwas, a theologian who is rightfully within a class of his own. For each of these three authors, we will provide a brief biographical sketch, as their personal narratives deeply influence their particular theological agendas that are driven by story and the 'storying' of the biblical text in the Church. In the third section, we will briefly mention 'other voices' that have made significant contributions in the postliberal theological dialogue. Some we discuss are more significant to the movement than others; and others may be more significant than the space we have allotted them. Nevertheless, either due to our own shortsightedness or the space limitations of this book, we will need to leave further research on these figures to our readers.

The Yale School: Hans Frei and George Lindbeck

The now common designation of 'Yale School' represents the basic approaches of postliberal theology or narrative theological approaches found in the work of various key theologians at Yale University and/or Divinity School. However, as most know, these specific 'parts' represent a greater whole to a movement that has become quite rich and diverse, spreading throughout various backgrounds and theological institutions. Of course, this does not discount the great significance of several key figures that remain points of departure for the movement as a whole. Among the many voices advocating a postliberal perspective in theology, perhaps the two most notable influences are George Lindbeck and Hans Frei. It is generally agreed that Frei's landmark book, *The Eclipse of Biblical Narrative*, followed by Lindbeck's, *The Nature of Doctrine*, set the stage for any theologian associated with or advocating a postliberal theology.

Hans Frei (1922–88)

Hans Frei may not be as well known as other theologians of the late twentieth century, but his influence is nonetheless extremely significant for the development of postliberal theological thought. Frei was born in Germany in 1922 to (non-devout) Jewish parents, both medical doctors and specialists. For his own safety during the rise of Nazism, he was sent to England to a Quaker school in 1935. It was here where he experienced Christianity, especially through the impact of a seeing a picture of Jesus. In 1938, Frei moved with his parents to New York. Frei studied textile engineering at North Carolina State University, but he shifted to the study of theology at Yale Divinity School, due to the influence of a lecture he heard by H. Richard Niebuhr, while he was at North Carolina State. Frei became an avid reader of theology during his studies at Yale. On graduation, he became a minister at a Baptist Church in New Hampshire, prior to returning to Yale University for his doctoral work under Niebuhr. Following the completion of his dissertation and various short teaching appointments, he was finally appointed to teach at Yale in 1958. It was here where the arduous research began for his most influential work, *The Eclipse of Biblical Narrative*.[1]

Frei's thorough and careful research demonstrates how theological readings of the Bible went drastically wrong in the seventeenth and eighteenth centuries. Enlightenment thinking created a perspective that changed the way people viewed the world – it became a place of constant scientific and rational inquiry. One's personal experience of this newly discovered rational universe took the driver's seat in all philosophical and theological inquiry. Modern theologies, likewise, attempted to form their theologies first from mankind's predicaments of existential despair, rather than from the Bible itself. Christianity became defended on the basis of human experience, external to the immediate context of the Christian faith. Modern philosophical questions provided the governing context for the interpretation of the biblical narrative; faith became subservient to culture. Frei echoed the same criticism of Barth: rather than this world of new sensibility fitting into the Bible, the Bible was seen as needing to fit into this modern world. The narrative of scripture became completely ignored and erased.[2] Frei put it this way in his famous statement: 'The great reversal had taken place; interpretation was a matter of fitting the biblical story into another world with another story rather than incorporating that world into the biblical story.'[3] Instead, the Bible should set the agenda and terms for the interpretation of our faith, not the world of modern experience.

Frei pointed out that the Bible no longer provided a special canon through which religious claims take their meaning that would not also 'make sense in a wider context of meaning'. At the same time, none who practised serious theological reflection wanted to suggest opposition to the application of biblical texts, 'once it had been determined what it was, even if one did not believe them on their own authority.' In light of these developments, it became not the case that these texts were devoid of meaning, but 'texts must have meaning in some way other than literal or factual.' This was played out in two basic ways according to Frei: supernaturalism and rationalism. This is noticed with respect to the interpretation of the gospel narratives. For supernaturalist theologians, the 'explicative and applicative meaning' was found in the historicity of Jesus as Messiah. The interest here is not so much with the text itself, but with reconstructing the context of that to which the text refers. For rationalists, however, the historical authenticity of the Gospels was insignificant compared to the mythological form of the Gospels, referring to the kernel truth of the love of God.[4]

Unfortunately, a faithful interpretation of the gospel narratives is wrongly neglected in each of these options. Both the super-naturalist and rationalist fail to see the story itself as significant, along with the characters and situations described.[5] As Frei puts it: 'Hermeneutics stood between religious apologetics and historical criticism, and these two worked against the narrative option ... the historian as such had no interest in applicative interpretation but only in explication.'[6] This problem is still evident today in debates between fundamentalist and liberal Christianity. Reinhold Niebuhr submitted that fundamentalism was mistaken because it took Christian myths literally, but liberalism was wrong because it did not take Christian myths seriously. Conservative apologists made every effort to prove the Christian narrative, without considering the full implications of the literary nature of the text. If the history is demonstrated as true, so they reason, then the narrative is true. The character of the narrative itself is neglected for the evidences behind the writing of the narrative. Contrariwise, theological liberals neglect the historical elements of the narrative in order to focus on the ethical and existential applications derived from the meaning behind the historical text. Both perspectives, according to Frei, betray the presupposition that the meaning of the Bible lies elsewhere than within the narrative of the biblical story itself – whether in historical, contextual evidences or within existential application. Either way, the biblical narrative, which should be our focus, becomes lost.[7] If we simply accommodate the Bible to a framework that seeks some larger meaning of the Bible for today, it ends up robbing scripture of the means by which it constitutes reality *for* itself. In order to remain scripturally faithful, we must see the Bible for itself – as a literary narrative that is consistent within itself. It is not subject to opposing narratives imposed on it. In fact, as Frei submits when referring to Barth, the Christian narrative *is* the common world 'in which we live and move and have our being'.[8]

The liberal, for Frei, has confused story or what he calls 'realistic narrative' with myth. The point of a myth is understood outside the narrative structure of the story itself. Myths are intended to convey archetypical aspects of truth for humanity and our existence in general. They personify abstract truth in the context of a narrative. However, the biblical narratives about Jesus cannot be classified in this manner. The biblical narratives are not simply used as stories to depict a universal truth, but they rather consist in and of themselves *as* truth. Although one may challenge Frei on whether indeed myth should be rendered with such separation of form and content in practice, his critique on liberal theology's appropriation of myth and its imposition on scriptural interpretation remains highly relevant. For Frei, in order to understand the realistic narrative of the Bible, one must not look toward an outside truth of either history or myth to gather its meaning, but strictly to the narrative itself. Meaning within the biblical narrative cannot be removed from the text; form and content are interwoven.[9] As Frei puts it: 'In a sense, every narrative of the sort in which story and meaning are closely related may have its own special hermeneutics.'[10] If the biblical narrative is interpreted according to modern principles of historiography then the form and content, the story and meaning, become disjointed. The same occurs if we reduce the Bible to the liberal rendering of myth. Instead, the biblical narrative must be embraced, appropriated and interpreted *as it is* in view of its own particular realistic character that maintains the integral unity of biblical story and meaning.

William Placher, summarizing Frei on this problem, suggests that if we begin with a modernist assumption of personal experience by first asking of the 'truth' of the biblical narrative, then the answer will only be affirmative if historical accuracy is confirmed or illustration is given pertaining to general human existence. Unfortunately, with good narratives, you cannot simply pull the lesson or 'meaning' from the narrative and do full justice to it. Simply trying to find a non-narrative deeper meaning to an existing narrative robs it of its character. So, Frei submits that we should not begin with the modern world, but we should begin with the world of the Bible, then let the narratives within the world of the Bible define reality on their own, rather than wrongly imposing a modern view of reality upon the Bible. The Bible's truth does not depend on externally imposed modernistic idea of the real world.[11]

As Geertz did with his ethnography of culture and semiotic systems, and Wittgenstein did with language games, so Frei submits that the Church is like a culture with its own scripture and grammar with rules that guide its participants as to its usage. The rules are more or less informal conventions learned in the context of application of scripture and all the flexibility that entails. Since scripture includes both Hebrew Bible and New Testament, the 'rules' must be lived and applied in view of this development. It is a mistake, however, if the rules become so rigid to demand that we only take the 'literal' sense of the Bible. Of course, the notion of 'literal' is ambiguous, and varies on its historical context. The literal sense of modernity came to mean simply literal description of events and historiography. The 'facts' of the matter became the governing paradigm of reality and the means by which one could bruise her opponents.[12]

Frei submits that there are various understandings on what the 'literal sense' actually means, and there are some 'rough rules' as to how it is to be defined. The first sense he suggests, drawing on the research of Charles Wood, pertains to its usage in the Church. The greatest degree of agreement within the religious community determines the literal sense of understanding. A second literal sense comes from understanding that texts are written by authors, with a relationship between the intentionality of the author(s) and the text itself. For Frei this means that we should not attempt to get behind a text to discover what an author *really* said or was attempting to say. The third basic understanding involves the descriptive correspondence between words and the subject matter. In terms of a question, we may ask: how does the structure of the text point to that which the text is speaking? It is under these guidelines that the discussion over 'literal sense' has taken shape, but it continues to change direction as literary readers mount an ongoing assault on the meaning of literary sense.[13] Frei elucidates this in his discussion of the failure of German realism:

But in the final analysis the precritical cohesion of historical reference with literal sense, rendering directly accessible the world literally depicted, came apart just as completely through dissolution into meaning as reference to the immanent development of events, and meaning as the development of a religious, interpretive stance and tradition. No matter to which side one gave priority, the meaning of the text was no longer the text's depiction, even if it was agreed that the text was indeed realistic in character. Its realistic character was identified either with its factual reliability or with a unique realistic spirit in the tradition that produced the text. These identifications, due to logical confusion between meaning and reference on the one hand and to religious-apologetical interests on the other, prevented the possibility of a straightforward appreciation of the biblical stories in their own right.[14]

It is this often manifested liberal–conservative divide with different base suppositions with respect to 'literalism' that continues to rupture the reality of the biblical narratives.

It is important to get to the heart of what Frei appears to be doing here. If theology simply concedes ground to Enlightenment categories of understanding alone, then the biblical narratives will always be interpreted through an external apologetic strategy, rather than allowing the narrative character of the Bible speak on its own terms, from its own internal grammar and linguistic integrity.[15] If 'literal' means simply signing up for a perspective on reality stemming from a modernist scientific and/or philosophical methodology, then we are correct in questioning that which is defined as literal. The questioning of what is literal in the text is not the same thing as questioning its grammatical integrity. For Frei, theology is:

> an inquiry into the internal logic of the Christian community's language—the rules, largely implicit rather than explicit, that are exhibited in its use in worship and Christian life, as well as in the confessions of Christian belief. Theology in other words, is the grammar of the religion, understood as a faith and as an ordered community life.[16]

But allowing the narrative of scripture to speak from its internal grammar must not be confused with method. For theology, theory must follow practice. In fact, Frei claims that he would prefer to trade method for character, since 'at heart' he does not 'believe in independent methodological study of theology'.[17] Perhaps another way to put it would be that true theology cannot be divorced from godliness in community.

Whether we are preoccupied with merely uncovering some sort of universal moral values, on one hand, or rigorously providing historically verifiable interpretations and authorial intentionality, on the other; both stray from a proper 'literal' understanding of scripture, and both ultimately fragment the unity of the canon. Both extremes end up imposing a distinctly separate standard of interpretation that is ultimately a modernist philosophical move external to the heart of the scriptural text. This is instructive to both theological liberals and conservative biblicists. Jesus must be seen and explained through the understanding of his life, death, resurrection and ongoing life in and through Christians. Jesus is both the character of the gospel narratives as well as the person Christians encounter through the sacraments. If Jesus is reduced to theological titles or viewed as some sort of existentially authentic model for humanity, or viewed in terms of other philosophical categories, than the Bible narratives are being robbed of their meaning.[18] D. Stephen Long points out that Frei (along with Thomas Aquinas) recognized the proper logic of the incarnation. They both understood that Jesus' identity is constant; he is one person in the hypostatic union of the human and divine. If we theologically divide the person of Jesus into a pre-Easter Jesus and a post-Easter Jesus, then we misrepresent the consistent narrative of scripture.[19] Further, if we philosophically over-theologize the 'hows' of this mysterious union, we will likewise stray from the purpose and intent of the biblical narrative.

It is important to remember that Frei is moving us to think less of the Bible as some sort of academic or historical sourcebook and more as a story to indwell. External logical structures from other disciplines that have been culturally or linguistically esteemed by a particular intellectual ethos should not be used as the barometer for the narratives of the Bible. For this would assume that there is some independent canon of reality to which the Bible must conform. Instead, the integrity of the internal linguistic reality of the Bible stands on its own.[20]

As we have noted already, Frei's work has significant implications for Christology. Frei argued that our Christian faith must begin with faithfulness to the unique narratives of the gospels to testify to the identity of Jesus as God incarnate, the crucified, risen Saviour. If we let modernist apologetics set the agenda, we can get so caught up with proving such things as the historical evidences for the resurrection, that we miss the identity and character of Jesus in the Gospel stories. The Gospels are neither pure history nor pure myth. Jesus must not be reduced to a mere piece of history to prove and examine, neither is he simply a mythological symbol. By simply giving systematic accounts and proofs for the Christian faith one ends up distorting and misrepresenting that faith.[21] Since the character of Jesus in the context of the community is central for faith, reducing it to proof related propositions distorts the intentions of that faith and wrongly places the emphasis on our own insights and understandings. Instead, Frei submits: 'To know Jesus one must indeed know who he is; and before he can be known, he must be able to withdraw from our grasp and turn to us from his own presence.'[22] Proofs and evidences are standards and expectations that come from a certain perspective of how reality is to be measured. But if the Christian faith is outside of that humanly imposed framework, it will not suffice to seek its compliance to these proposed standards of evaluation that have arisen not from Christian necessity but from modernist historiography.

In Frei's work, *The Identity of Jesus Christ* (orig. pub. 1975), he emphasizes Jesus' identity over his presence. Theological discussions in Christology often focus on the Christology from above or Christology from below debates with respect to how Jesus presence is mediated, and in what sense and to what degree. For Frei, if we know the identity of Jesus, it is the same as having him present with us. That is, understanding Jesus' identity is identical with him being present. This is especially true with regard to the Gospels; if the Gospels are understandable, then the identity of Jesus rendered in the gospel narratives must indeed live as well.[23]

Frei claims that there is an inextricable connection between presence and body. It makes no sense, unless you are a spiritualist, to suggest that you know a person unless that person has been present in bodily form at a particular location. And we may continue to think of a person's presence even after the person has departed from our direct presence. However, this does not work for the Christian claim about Jesus Christ's personal presence since he is not actually present with us in this fashion today. At the same time, we cannot think of Christ without his presence with us in some manner. But for Frei this has nothing to do with our ability to think of his presence and thus make him present, it is rather about Christ making his presence known to us. His unity and identity are made known to us only by His act of making it known. This is not simply imposing an imaginative rendering of presence onto the common understanding of being present. This is a troublesome mystery to the nonbeliever, since it is unlike normal knowledge of human relationships. Jesus' presence is manifested differently than in mere categories of space and time. For example, Christ's sacramental presence is considered 'real' even though it is not rendered as 'physical' presence. It may be the closest thing we have to physical presence, but it certainly is not equal to it. For Christ is indeed present with us 'always and already' according to his promise to be with us always 'to the end of the age' (Matt. 28.20). For Frei, then, Jesus presence is a formal, yet very proper way to discuss the relationship that he has with Christian believers.[24]

If we return to Frei's initial observation as to the meaning of presence always being associated with physical, bodily presence, then the question also arises as to whether Jesus' presence with us depends on a literal, physical resurrection. For Frei, is physical resurrection absolutely significant or is it equally significant to think of the resurrection event of Christ in a symbolic fashion? Frei seems to avoid a direct answer to this question. On this subject, Frei had an interesting and well-known exchange with the evangelical theologian, Carl F. H. Henry, on the matter of the reality of the 'empty tomb' of Jesus. Henry pressed Frei for an answer as to whether this event was indeed a 'fact'. In response, Frei made the following remarks:

> If I am asked to use the language of factuality, then I would say, yes, in those terms, I have to speak of an empty tomb. In those terms I have to speak of a literal resurrection. But I think those terms are not privileged, theory-neutral, transcultural, an ingredient in the structure of the human mind and of reality always and everywhere for me, as I think they are for Dr. Henry. Now that may mean, you see, that I am looking for a way that doesn't exist between evangelicalism on the one hand and liberalism on the other. If that's the case, well, so be it. But it may also be that I am looking for a way that looks for a relation between Christian theology and philosophy that disagrees with a view of certainty and knowledge which liberals and evangelicals hold in common.[25]

Indeed, Frei agrees that the resurrection must definitely be affirmed by Christians as something that really occurred. But for Frei, as to the question on whether it was literal or symbolic, neither points to the nature of Christ's presence with us now, which is more critical for our understanding. If we pursue arguments along these lines, such as evidential arguments for Christ's bodily resurrection, they will not be of help to our faith. Furthermore, such efforts will trap us into a way of viewing presence that is reductionist and modern, distracting us from the richness of his real presence with us and diffusing His presence into our own. Instead, as we mentioned earlier, Frei is suggesting that the term 'presence' is a formal designation and unique for Christians and their particular relationship with Christ. It will ultimately not make sense to the unbeliever who maintains a more limited definition of presence from personal experience apart from Christ. We want to be clear on this point. Frei is by no means denying the historicity of a bodily resurrection of Jesus; in fact, he claims that this 'temporal basis' of Christ's presence 'must be grasped through the imagination' even perhaps with the resources of historical research. But, for Frei, we should not base our belief in the presence of Christ uniquely on the imaginative re-creation of such events of Christ's temporality.[26]

Nonetheless, we cannot help but wonder if Frei sells himself a bit short on the importance of the physical resurrection of Christ with regard to presence. Must the notion of 'presence' remain a formal designation? Frei admits from the beginning that the most basic understanding of presence involves bodily, spatial presence. Is this not a critical point of the incarnation? Jesus was born, he lived, he died and he rose again in a physical body. We would suggest that this is absolutely essential to the Jesus narrative and must be embraced as such. But simply stressing the absolute importance of bodily resurrection does not necessarily imply that we must employ modernist historical arguments to prove its occurrence. At the same time, it does not negate the more sacramental, mystical, 'real' side to Christ's presence with us that Frei appears to be afraid of losing if the literal, historical aspect of presence is stressed. We believe that a healthy, strong postliberal theology should affirm both a literal, bodily resurrection *and* its symbolic call towards sacramental, no less 'real' presence. Jesus resurrected in body, but granted, it was a body that could cross into another 'spiritual dimension' per se, since he is now present with the Father in heaven. At the same time, Jesus mediates his presence to us (this is where the more mystical, imaginative aspect comes into play) via the Holy Spirit, until the day of the Parousia when his bodily presence will again be made fully manifest to us.

We see the obvious influence of Karl Barth on the shaping of
Frei's perspectives in *Types of Christian Theology*. Barth is listed as
Frei's theology 'Type 4,' as we briefly discussed in our introductory
chapter. Frei claims that it is very clear with Barth that the meaning
of Christian propositions does not lie in their reference. Christian
theology's priority is about critical self-reflection. It is not based
on philosophy, and its order does not come from some external
universal principles that lay claim on its justification. Instead, Frei
claims, for Barth theology uses its own set of implicit rules by
which it is legitimized as a field of investigation. Theology is the
concern and responsibility of the Church.[27] He provides this lucid
summary of his understanding of Barth's view of theology:

> Theology as specific and critical Christian self-description and
> self-examination by the Church of its language takes absolute
> priority over theology as an academic discipline. Philosophy
> as conceptual system describing and referring to 'reality' is not
> a basis on which to build theology, and even philosophy as a
> set of formal, universal rules or criteria for what may count
> as coherent and true in Christian discourse as in every other
> kind of conceptual practice is not basic to or foundational of
> Christian theology.[28]

So for Barth prolegomena is not about the ultimate principles or
foundational methods for doing dogmatic theology, neither is it
some overarching umbrella by which to evaluate theological propositions, but it is an integral part of dogmatic theology itself.[29] Barth
practised what he preached by using a narrative technique in his
Church Dogmatics, providing descriptions rather than arguments
or logical explanations. The world Barth described was a biblical
world with its own language and literature, not dependent on an
external philosophical gatekeeper. It is the world, in fact, in which
we all live and exist and a world that is 'descriptively accessible'.[30]

Frei most certainly drew on Barth in his personal reflections
with respect to biblical hermeneutics. The Bible is full of stories
containing real narratives describing events and occurrences of
people. These stories cannot simply be reduced to fables with
moral lessons, but neither can they be put through the rigours of
historicism. William Placher spells this out clearly with regard to
Frei's understanding of the past 200 years of biblical hermeneutics.

Placher points out that if we begin with modernist assumptions and ask about whether or not the stories in the Bible are true, the answer may only be in the affirmative if the stories report historical information or if they give moral examples for human living. Since scholars embracing a modern scientific paradigm could not embrace the historical accuracy of the Bible, then by logical deduction the stories must be reduced to moral narratives about our human existence. Frei offers a brilliant solution to this conundrum. If we choose not to begin with our modernist assumptions and biases, but instead allow the biblical world to speak for itself, allowing its own narrative to define reality rather than modernism, then an entirely new theological world is opened up to us. This, in fact, for Frei, would describe the real world.[31] We should not be about the business of fitting the world of the Bible and theology into another 'self' created world of science, historicism, and modernist philosophy, but instead we must let the world of the Bible speak for itself, in and through its own world and linguistic and cultural integrity.

We should not misunderstand Frei's understanding and assimilation of Barth as a mere concession to a 'Wittgensteinian fideism' such as that represented by D. Z. Phillips, who believed theology to be exclusively an internal activity of the community.[32] Rather, Frei acknowledges that Barth would engage in ad hoc apologetics to show how various aspects of the narrated world of the Bible were indeed similar or different than descriptions drawn from other linguistic worlds. In this fashion, Frei observes, Barth would engage in dialectical argument 'to indicate distance and proximity at the same time'. However, Barth would never use these arguments as support for some sort of pre-description or prolegomena for the narrative world of Christian discourse.[33] Certainly Frei (as well as Barth) understood that we do not simply read scripture in a total vacuum either. We need some concepts for arranging the categories of our understanding. We cannot be freed from our 'own shadow' and assume a 'view from nowhere' prior to taking up the scriptural narrative. Frei would also not create a false dichotomy between indwelling the narrative of the Bible and discovering truths of the world portrayed by different theological expressions derived independently. Like Barth, Frei's apologetic efforts are ad hoc rather than systematic.[34]

By simply stating that Frei is not a 'Wittgensteinian fideist', however, is not to say that he was not deeply influenced by

Wittgenstein. Jason Springs effectively cites two major influences that Wittgenstein had on Frei's theology. First of all, Wittgenstein weaned Frei from thinking he needed one specialized grammar for theology and philosophy together. These are separate disciplines that require their own rules of use. The second is related to the first, in that Wittgenstein challenged Frei to move away from thinking he needed rigorous ontological musings in order to understand theology.[35] Further, in several essays written by Frei in the 1960s, both Wittgenstein and Clifford Geertz showed a marked influence on him as he described the narrative of the identity of Christ and the sociology of church practices and their contexts.

Frei's desire was ultimately to preserve the Bible from modern influences that would distort the way that it should be read. His theology, like that of Barth, is a theology within and for the Church. The narrative of the Bible is to shape the Church, and be used by the Church to shape its understanding of the world. But Frei made no presumptions that he had answered all the difficult questions. Certainly, the Bible is not simply one story, but includes many stories and narratives and genres. Frei most likely would have admitted that he simply could not solve all these issues. Regardless, his contributions and insights are clear and provoking.[36] We have, of course, only barely scratched the surface on Frei's brilliant observations and contributions to our understanding of theology and biblical narrative, but we trust this has provided a springboard for our further investigations into the core developments of postliberal theology.

George Lindbeck (1923–)

Although the stage was certainly set for postliberal theology by Barth and followed by Frei's appropriation of Barth, the term 'postliberal' itself is not duly considered until the publication of George Lindbeck's short but extremely influential book, *The Nature of Doctrine: Religion and Theology in a Postliberal Age* (1984).[37] Even in this book, excluding the subtitle, the word itself only surfaces in his final chapter. Lindbeck, a colleague of Frei, expands on Frei's intratextualism, and borrows narrative hermeneutic ingredients from both Frei and David Kelsey, and applies both the linguistic analysis of Wittgenstein joined with the cultural anthropology of Geertz.[38] However, as David Tracy argues: 'Lindbeck's substantive theological position is a methodologically sophisticated version of Barthian confessionalism. The hands may be the hands of Wittgenstein and Geertz, but the voice is the voice of Karl Barth.'[39] Lindbeck extends Frei's criticism into a theological proposal to promote ecumenical unity through a cultural–linguistic approach to religion.[40] Lindbeck forthrightly claims that his ideas were 'mostly borrowed', 'pretheological' and his approach is 'ad hoc and unsystematic', which conforms to 'Barth's recommendations for the employment of non-scriptural concepts in theology and to contemporary anti-foundational trends in Anglo-American philosophy'.[41]

Before we specifically discuss Lindbeck's proposals, it may be helpful to briefly set the context for his work by providing some biographical notes. Lindbeck was born in China in 1923 to parents who were American Lutheran missionaries. As a child, Lindbeck was quite sickly, so he never learned the Chinese language well. However, he was captivated by the literature he found on ancient Luoyang, the city of his birth. He read about many buried ruins in this ancient imperial city capital of China. At its zenith, the first 200 years after Christ, Luoyang rivalled Rome in population. During his reading, Lindbeck became astonished regarding the stark difference between Luoyang's triumphant past and current condition. Nevertheless, it made a deep impression on Lindbeck that there remained some significant continuities between the past and present worlds of this city. One example Lindbeck recalls was exemplified in some close Chinese friends of his parents, a pastor and his wife. Lindbeck noted that this couple was 'warmly Christian' but in their manners they were 'Confucian to the core'. These observations made a deep-seated impression on Lindbeck that developed his four basic convictions that are the basic ingredients of his cultural–linguistic view of religion, which is a scripture–narrative focused view of Christianity and a grammar based theory of doctrine.[42]

First of all, Lindbeck noticed that our communal context shapes who we are 'more than we shape ourselves'. Second, Lindbeck suggests that the basics of being human are very similar in all cultures. Third, and perhaps ironically, despite such similarities in our humanness, our particular cultures and languages prevent effective communication. Fourth, and most importantly for

Lindbeck, communities that are 'book sustained,' that is communities that create systems of thought and practice, are able to stand strong against various onslaughts of social, political, economic, and linguistic upheaval.[43] As we look a bit closer at Lindbeck's thought, we will see how these forms of thinking greatly influenced his postliberal version of theology.

At age 17, Lindbeck left for university studies in the United States. He earned a BA degree in 1943 from Adolphus College in Minnesota, a premier-status Lutheran institution of higher learning. He then continued his education at Yale Divinity School and earned a Bachelor of Divinity degree in 1946. This was followed by a year at the Pontifical Institute of Medieval Studies in Toronto and two years at the École Pratique des Hautes Études in Paris. During this time his interests in Lutheran–Roman Catholic dialogue were heightened. No doubt these studies, combined with his background of being firmly rooted in his Lutheran faith while in constant dialogue with various traditions, cultures and backgrounds, mitigated to spur his interests forward. In 1955, after already teaching at Yale, he finished his PhD (also at Yale) with research on the medieval Franciscan theologian, Duns Scotus.[44] As he began teaching with Hans Frei, Paul Holmer, and David Kelsey, the stage was set for his pivotal book for postliberal theology: *The Nature of Doctrine*.

Lindbeck's early work in the area of medieval Catholic theology prompted his delegation as a representative at the Lutheran World Federation at Vatican II. These four sessions of the Council were decisive for Lindbeck in terms of his future ecumenical interests. His deep ecumenical interests accompanied by his engagement in a series of dialogues also fired an interest in his thinking of a new approach to Christian doctrine. Lindbeck submitted that we need a clearer way to understand the nature and intent of doctrines because they are not functioning in the ways they should with our contemporary mindset. He expresses this forthrightly in the foreword to *The Nature of Doctrine*:

It has become apparent to me, during twenty-five years of involvement in ecumenical discussions and in teaching about the history and present status of doctrines, that those of us who are engaged in these activities lack adequate categories for conceptualizing the problems that arise. We are often unable, for example, to specify the criteria we implicitly employ when we say that some changes are faithful to a doctrinal tradition and others unfaithful, or some doctrinal differences are church-dividing and others not.[45]

With this concern in mind, let us turn to what Lindbeck proposed as way forward from the conservative/liberal impasse.

Lindbeck submitted that there are three basic approaches to religion and doctrine. The one that is typical of traditional ortho-doxies and heterodoxies is the cognitive–propositional approach, which has affinities to Anglo-American analytic philosophy. This approach stresses 'factual' information and the meaningfulness of theological statements and their truth claims with respect to objective reality. Another approach is what Lindbeck calls 'experi-ential–expressive'. Doctrines are interpreted not as information, but are seen subjectively as symbols revealing existential orienta-tions or feelings. Unfortunately, both of these approaches have capitulated to a modernist mentality that gives to much ground to rationalism and empiricism.[46]

The third approach is a hybrid of the first two and is especially recognized by ecumenical Roman Catholics. Both the propositional and symbolic characteristics of doctrine are seen as theologically important for the Christian religion. Lindbeck claims that Karl Rahner and Bernard Lonergan are premier examples of those implementing this approach. Unfortunately, however, with these three approaches Lindbeck finds little hope of ecumenical reconcili-ation without one perspective finally capitulating to another. Unless one perspective abandons an earlier position, ultimately harmony in doctrinal understanding is not possible.[47]

With the cognitive–propositional approach doctrines are seen as either true or false and will always remain thus. Changes cannot be made without the abandonment of propositional meaning. By way of contrast, for those holding an experiential–expressive approach, *meanings* can certainly change while the actual doctrines remain unaltered, and vice versa. Symbols themselves are not critical for theological harmony because they refer to feelings or attitudes existentially.[48] William Placher points out that for Lindbeck, the experiential–expressivist approach inverses the relation between experience and language. It is not that we first have an experience then try to find the language by which to express the experience.

Instead, it is language that makes complex human experience even possible. Language shapes the character of experience. As Placher puts it: 'Therefore, prelinguistic experience can hardly provide the criterion for judging linguistic formulations. We cannot argue for Christianity by saying that it best captures the essence of universal religiousness, since there is no coherent "religiousness" prior to a particular tradition's language.'[49]

The third hybrid approach may seem at first like a worthy option, but in reality would require 'complicated intellectual gymnastics' that makes its viability unconvincing. For example, how would Roman Catholics neglect ultimate dependence on the magisterium and still promote ecumenical harmony with Protestant theology? In theory, this approach is certainly more ecumenically minded than propositional or symbolic approaches, but its application seems much too difficult to implement. So Lindbeck suggests another alternative to make the 'intertwining of variability and invariability in matters of faith easier to understand'.[50] This provides the entry point to Lindbeck's cultural–linguistic approach to theology that characterizes his postliberalism.

A cultural–linguistic approach to theology, Lindbeck submits, takes into account a comprehensive view of our humanity in terms of anthropology, sociology, and philosophy, along with the complete organization of our experience and beliefs. A cultural–linguistic framework also allows for a description of beliefs, the experience of emotions, and the grammar by which such things can be expressed. As Wittgenstein's language games correspond to a particular aspect of life, so both cultures and religious traditions have both aspects of cognition and behaviour. The doctrines, stories and ethics of a religious tradition are integrally related to its practices. When we become Christians, we learn the story of the Bible and interpret our own lives through the lens of that story. And this story, for Lindbeck, is not simply about statements or propositions that we affirm, but it is a story involving skills, practices and symbols that govern the reality of our lives.[51] William Placher suggests that a 'good Lindbeckian, postliberal theologian will therefore operate less like a philosophically oriented apologist and more like a sensitive anthropologist.' Instead of being devoted to defending some overarching human rationality to defend a belief system, Lindbeck seeks to describe how the language practices of the Christian community function in that community and how it shapes the way it views the world. In Wittgensteinian fashion, Lindbeck's approach contends that meaning is integrally linked to the language game or particular contexts in which words function, and their practices related to the speech act.[52]

So religion, in this cultural–linguistic model, is not simply about believing certain statements to be true. Religion involves deeply interiorizing the rituals and skills of the cultural–linguistic community. With Christianity then, truth claims are not based primarily on cognitive factors, but rather on Christianity's own particular vocabulary and inner logic. Through the participation in the practice of these rituals and skills in the complete context of the community the gospel is proclaimed and passed along.[53] As Lindbeck adds: 'The primary knowledge is not *about* the religion, nor *that* the religion teaches such and such, but rather *how* to be religious in such and such ways.'[54] The cognitive–propositional perspective examines doctrine in terms of technical theological statements, whereas Lindbeck's cultural– linguistic approach look at religious language as it shapes lives through such things as prayer and preaching. It is through these areas of Christian practice that correspondence to truth is made manifest. In this case, technical and propositional theological expression is viewed as 'second-order discourse' about the first-order practice of religious language. Just as the grammar of a language does not in itself make truth claims about the world in which the language functions, so also this second-order discourse and doctrine does not affirm the truth or falsity of religious assertions but only speaks about them.[55]

We must not misunderstand Lindbeck at this point. It is not that our religious claims are completely void of cognitive truth claims or experiences, but these are not the primary functions of Christian doctrine. Rather, doctrines express the framework and grammar of the community, providing the basic framework for communication within that community. We are linguistically and historically shaped as human beings within the particular experience of our culture. The confessional faith of the church that stems from the narrative of the Bible is what shapes the cultural and linguistic world in which we live. So our focus should be on optimizing and improving this internal linguistic structure that stands on its own terms. It is not about somehow standing outside our community then evaluating it from a neutral viewpoint with some universally accepted standards; instead, it is about practising and living the rules from within our community.[56]

There are a couple of examples from Lindbeck that make this clear. When Christians make the claim that 'Jesus is Lord', it is most fully meaningful when the utterance expresses one's complete commitment in community to the lordship of Christ. This is not simply a cognitive proposition intended to be analyzed or stated without personal or communal experiential force; neither can it be simply reduced to a symbol of experience. It is a proposition *and* it is experiential *and* a symbol of that experience, and more. By both *uttering* and by *performing* the claim, its meaning comes to complete fruition.[57]

Lindbeck also provides an interesting parallel to his cultural–linguistic approach with an example of what he considers the 'modest propositionalism' of Aquinas. For Aquinas, when we make statements about God as humans, our finiteness prevents us from making any direct signifying utterances about the Divine. For instance, if we say that God is good, our notions of goodness cannot directly apply to God, but there is nonetheless a concept of goodness based on God's understanding of himself that would apply to God being good. Analogies are often used not to make definitive affirmations, but to demonstrate how certain statements may not make expected affirmations of reality. Although we may agree that the cognitive content of such an assertion may be weak, our understanding of it as expressed in our faith narrative community is still vital. God's goodness is witnessed in his creation and providence, as well as through his acts of redemption. These acts of goodness have impacted our perspectives and practices of faith. We should not attempt to analyze God's innate goodness from some 'objective' standpoint outside our faith, but always within the context of our faith.[58]

One final example cited by William Placher in order to illustrate Lindbeck's position may be helpful. If we take the theological pronouncement, 'We are saved by grace alone', it will be understood by propositionalists as a statement of fact with regard to the way by which we receive salvation and forgiveness from the Lord. But the experiential–expressivist may understand this more as a symbolic way to describe the power of God in our lives. For Lindbeck, however, the meaning would be more akin to a rule demanding as Christians that we should always demonstrate gratefulness in our actions toward God, rather than taking credit for our own achievements.[59] It becomes clear through these examples that Lindbeck sees doctrinal assertions as actions expressed within the context and practice of the Christian community, rather than simply as factual statements or mere symbols.

Lindbeck provides three doctrinal rules stemming from the early church and the time of the New Testament that are necessary, although not completely sufficient for defining Christianity. The first is monotheism. The second is the belief in the historical particularity of Jesus as a human being who lived and died. The third, Lindbeck calls 'Christological maximalism', meaning that Jesus is central to everything in human experience, as long as it does not conflict with the first two doctrinal rules. Lindbeck acknowledges that other rules (some important and some not so important) are also important for the Christian faith, but these three doctrinal rules are essential.[60] Lindbeck states the following relating these 'rules' to the creeds of Nicene and Chalcedon: 'These creeds can be understood by Christian and non-Christian alike as paradigmatically instantiating doctrinal rules that have been abidingly important from the beginning in forming mainstream Christian identity.'[61] However, Lindbeck clarifies that his argument is not that the early Christians used these essential three 'rules' any more than when those speaking their native tongue consciously follow the rules of their language.[62] The 'rules' are simply followed by years of an embedded practice and habit of speech. The point here is that the principles are embedded in the religious practices of the early Christians and are therefore also essential characteristics for the definition of Christianity today.

In the foreword to the German edition of *The Nature of Doctrine*, published ten years after the English edition, Lindbeck expanded his thinking on this matter significantly, integrating the relationship between Israel and Church more profoundly. In fact, the way in which he describes this change of perspective is a good example of a postliberal understanding of how doctrine continues to shape the narrative of the church: 'This is not the book it was 10 years ago when it was first published. It was captured by unanticipated interest groups who so shaped the public reception that even I, the author, now read it partly through their eyes.'[63] We are reminded of the dialectic between language and culture emphasized with Clifford Geertz and that of individuals and society stressed by Peter Berger. Similarly, we have noticed the interrelationship between the Church community and the formation of Christian doctrine. Doctrine shapes the Church and the experience of the Church community through the Holy Spirit, which in turn shapes (and reshapes?) the expression of doctrine.

In the German edition foreword, Lindbeck strongly affirmed the need to begin a comparative dogmatics with an ecclesiology that is an 'Israel-ology.' A truly holistic scriptural narrative approach must necessarily include Israel. For Lindbeck, both Israel and the Church are God's one elect people; and both are integrally linked in the Bible where the God of Israel and Jesus are the authorities of the respective communities.[64] Christians must integrate the story of Israel into the Christian narrative without promoting a replacement theology or implying triumphalism. We are called to serve, not advocate a privileged position. In view of modernity's demise, for Lindbeck, Christians must move closer to premodernity by retrieving 'critically and repentantly, the heritage in the Hebrew scriptures, apostolic writings and early tradition'.[65] This Christian retrieval of the importance of Israel, the bringing together of God's people from Jew to Gentile, will model true ecumenical unity for a diverse postmodern world.

Lindbeck and Frei

Gary Dorrien suggested that Lindbeck's proposals in *The Nature of Doctrine* 'reinforced and amplified' much of the argument started by Hans Frei.[66] However, postliberal theologian George Hunsinger seems to disagree, at least in principle. Both Frei and Lindbeck were influenced by Wittgenstein, but Lindbeck was much more pragmatic in his agenda than Frei. Frei relied on Barth for this theological direction, but Lindbeck relied more on Aquinas and Luther. Lindbeck, Hunsinger argues, suggested a notion of truth that depended on religious practice, whereas Frei was more moderate in his perspective on proposition-alism. He points out that Frei, unlike Lindbeck, did not draw a sharp distinction between first- and second-order theological discourse, but rather between first- and second-level functions. Moreover, Frei would not see second-level functions as simply regulative. For Frei, truth claims can be made even at the grammatical or propositional level.[67] Frei elucidates this when he writes:

Theology in the first sense has philosophy for its natural cognate discipline, especially transcendental philosophy, and because transcendental philosophy claims to provide the theoretical justification of all of all explanation (Wissenschaftstheorie), theology is accountable to it. In effect, it is a subdiscipline of philosophy which provides it with its criteria of meaning and truth and, of course, with its academic organization. No matter what theology may entail logically in practical consequences, it is vocationally the profession of an intellectual, a theorist.[68]

This quotation certainly does not carry the same overriding pragmatic tone that we find in Lindbeck. It is not the case that Frei ignores theology as religious practice, as this is part of learning its grammar in its semiotic system. But for Frei the theory *itself* is part of the practice, 'the ruled practice of culture' by those who understand the rules and traditions of their social context.[69]

Jeannine Fletcher also points out the parallel thinking between Lindbeck and Thomas Kuhn. Different paradigms of community life may obfuscate conversational contact. Since different paradigms with different systems of language render and organize reality differently, it restricts the shape of the expression of what may be known about reality. So, people from different frameworks or paradigms will in effect 'talk through each other'. This does not imply, however, as Fletcher astutely points out, that such incommensurability implies a total inability for Lindbeck to communicate across differing paradigms. Effective communication can occur if one is able to adopt or inhabit another paradigm since it is impossible converse with unbiased neutrality. One must live within a paradigm in order to understand it and achieve understanding. This is what Lindbeck calls, borrowing from Alasdair MacIntyre, 'genuine bilingualism'.[70] Fletcher expands this notion as to how such bilingualism may be achieved in Lindbeckian fashion.[71]

It is the contention of this book, however, that the pursuit of such bilingualism betrays already a lingering notion of presumed neutrality. If one truly embraces a paradigm and lives according to its practices with devotion within a community of faith, to suggest that one essentially adopts a differing paradigm in order to achieve conversational contact also seems to assume one may continue to embrace that faith while keeping his or her lenses clear enough to see the differing faith or paradigm from within that particular faith or paradigm. Granted, Fletcher (as she develops this in the work of Francis Clooney) submits that this requires great diligence and tenacity to achieve such rare bilingual adeptness, but she nevertheless asserts its possibility. We will briefly return to a variation of this critique in a later chapter.

The community ethics of
Stanley Hauerwas

Stanley Hauerwas was the son of a Methodist bricklayer, born in Pleasant Grove, Texas on July 24, 1940. From his blue-collar origins and rigorous work ethic, he was eventually heralded as America's 'best theologian' by *Time* magazine just prior to September 11, 2001. Although Hauerwas would be reticent to flag the 'best theologian' title, he credits his given notoriety not from his innate brilliance, but due to his values of hard, diligent work that he learned as an apprentice working with his father and uncles. Hauerwas recounts his background and most notable influences in his recent autobiographical work, *Hannah's Child: A Theologian's Memoir* (Eerdmans, 2010). He was raised a devout Methodist, and committed his life to ministry at the age of 15 at a Sunday evening worship gathering with a long alter call. He went on to study theology because he said he wanted to 'get saved' but it 'just didn't happen'. So he thought if he dedicated his life to ministry then he would 'put God under some constraint'.[72] Hauerwas would carry his working-class rigour and his direct, often colourful vocabulary into the halls of the theological academy.

The first in his family to attend college, Hauerwas left the bricks of Texas for the books of Southwestern University, a liberal arts school associated with the Methodist Church. When he began his university studies, he did not consider himself a Christian anymore, but in his reading of philosophy, he could not be convinced of atheism either. After reading H. Richard Niebuhr's, *The Meaning of Revelation*, he was compelled to go to Yale Divinity School to find out 'if that stuff was true'.[73] In this pursuit, he earned multiple degrees in theology and philosophy, culminating in the PhD. Hauerwas went on to teach at Augustana College in Illinois, the University of Notre Dame, then on to his current position at

Duke University in 1983, where he is currently the Gilbert T. Rowe Professor of Theological Ethics, holding a joint appointment at the Duke University School of Law.

Despite his title 'America's best theologian', Hauerwas is by no means a typical American patriot. Hauerwas is known for his outspoken pacifism and anti-capitalist sentiments and he believes that the 'God that is called forward to God Bless America is not the God of Jesus Christ.'[74] It is evident in Hauerwas's writings that he believes that being committed to American patriotic ideals is not tantamount to being committed to Jesus and the church; in fact, it may be just the opposite in many cases.

Hauerwas is theologically orthodox but he is highly critical of both biblicistic conservatism and theological liberalism. He believes he is disliked by conservatives because he refuses to allow Christian salvation be influenced by the presuppositions of 'American' individualism and democratic ideals. But liberals also find him distasteful because of his insistence on an unapologetic theology.[75]

Where Frei emphasized the vocabulary of 'narrative', Stanley Hauerwas speaks of 'stories'. Essentially, they are the same. For Hauerwas, the church is the extended story of Christ's activity in the world. Our Christian story in community points us in the right direction for living as God's people. As the community of Christ, we embody His story and manifest that story to the world. Moving Frei's work forward, Hauerwas links Christian identity to the activity of Christians in community embodying Christ to the world. It is not that Christians make their own individual story, but they participate in the ongoing and unfolding story of Christianity throughout history. Hauerwas effectively critiques liberalism, like Frei and Lindbeck, by combining the cultural–linguistic approach of Lindbeck with the Mennonite, pacifist ecclesiology of his mentor, John Howard Yoder.[76] Jesus is not to be seen as simply holding to a social ethic that we must seek to recover; Jesus himself *is* a social ethic. For the Christian community to be both socially and politically valid, it must be shaped by a truthful story. That truthful story is the story of Jesus himself, other saviour stories will not do. The moral message of Jesus cannot be separated from the Jesus of the Gospels. Jesus is uniquely both the Christ and Saviour, hence he cannot be considered apart from both his incarnation and his atoning work. The only way to understand the Kingdom of God and participate as a disciple in God's rule, in God's new community, is to learn and share the story of Jesus.[77] As Hauerwas adds: 'Therefore there can be no separation of christology from ecclesiology, that is, Jesus from the church. The truthfulness of Jesus creates and is known by the kind of community his story should form.'[78]

Consequently, for Hauerwas, the job of the church community is to 'tell and live' the story of Jesus truthfully to the world. This does not mean that we should be about the business of reconstructing some exacting historical account of what Jesus exactly did from the gospels. Rather, we must realize that Jesus' life is inextricably linked to how we must live as well. This is not a one size fits all, cookie-cutter approach to the story of Jesus. As there are four diverse Gospels, so there are various stories and approaches to the story of Jesus. The exact account is not the point; the point is that as Christians we are the ongoing truth of the Kingdom of God as we diligently strive in community to be faithful to the Gospel by demonstrating love to each other.[79] Hauerwas will neither tolerate the vague, universal ethics of theological liberalism along with its higher critical methods, nor does he have patience for the literalism advocated by theological fundamentalism. The narratives of the Gospels are extremely important for what they are: the story of Jesus. But the story of Jesus in turn becomes the story that shapes our Christian community.

Ironically, in one of Hauerwas' latest works, he disdains the title of 'narrative theologian'. In fact, any qualifier to his theology other than simply the word 'Christian' is viewed with suspicion by Hauerwas, because it suggests that a particular theory of theology may be esteemed as more important than God himself. His concern is that if narrative is viewed as merely an apologetic endeavour, it may unintentionally result in a misappropriated focus on the 'sovereign self' that dominates modern thought.[80] Of course, his entire point is contra the 'sovereign self' and pro-community. He is not simply emphasizing our personal stories, but rather the story of Jesus in the Gospels and how *our* stories flow from that unique and particular story. Hauerwas is in no way countering his earlier mentioned claims as to the importance of narrative, but he is opposed to linking narrative to an apologetic strategy that may be used to support a universal anthropological understanding of the human condition.[81] Viewing narrative as a theological or apologetic system is fundamentally different than viewing narrative as the story of the person of Jesus Christ, who is not most essentially about proclaiming the truth, but who *is* the truth.

In this regard, Hauerwas was greatly influenced by the Mennonite theologian John Howard Yoder. Certainly Jesus proclaims the Kingdom of God, but more significantly he *is* the very presence of the Kingdom of God. Jesus expresses and is the Kingdom in both what he proclaims and what he does. Likewise, as Christians we are not called simply to proclaim the Kingdom, but we are to be the reality of the Kingdom of God as we locate ourselves, in community within his Kingdom. As Jesus *is* a social ethic, so we also *are* a social ethic. However, to be a social ethic is not about autonomy, but about community and disciplined faithfulness to a truthful story.[82] Practically, this will be expressed through simple acts of kindness that promote justice and peace. Hauerwas aptly expresses this challenge: 'We must be a community with the patience, amid the division and hatreds of this world, to take the time to nurture friendships, to serve the neighbor, and to give and receive the thousand small acts of care that ultimately are the heart blood of the Kingdom.'[83]

Hauerwas was also deeply influenced by the pragmatism of Lindbeck's cultural–linguistic emphasis, along with virtue ethics of Alasdair MacIntyre. He enthusiastically approved of Lindbeck's stress on religion not being primarily about true or false propositions, but about skills and practices for living. But where Lindbeck's cultural–linguistic approach emphasized religious language as the possibility for religious life, Hauerwas emphasizes stories in Christian community as creating possibilities for various expressions of the virtuous life. As Alasdair MacIntyre linked personal life narratives with an entire set of narratives situated in communities from which one's personal identity is derived, so Hauerwas links Christian action to the narrative of Christian community.[84]

Hauerwas, like MacIntyre, is known to be highly critical of modernism. He believes that modernism forgets our finite human nature and attempts to simply wipe clean a slate that cannot be wiped clean, convincing its followers that they can simply create their own stories. Similar to both Frei and Lindbeck, Hauerwas is reacting against the ongoing divide against propositional fundamentalism and higher critical approaches to biblical interpretation stemming from modernity. Both approaches, for Hauerwas, share the same modernist assumptions of rationalism and common sense realism as universal, overarching arbiters of truth. Both seek to make the text of the Bible objective truth. This, however, hands scripture over to an unchecked, unjustified power of politics that misgoverns biblical interpretation. Both higher criticism and fundamentalism assume the Enlightenment notion of the objective, rational individual who can obtain truth apart from the ethical context of the community. Hauerwas links the cause of this gross misunderstanding to a misapplication of the reformation doctrine of *sola scriptura* accompanied by the invention of the printing press.[85] If the distinction between text and interpretation is made under the notion of *sola scriptura*, then it becomes a heresy. As Hauerwas argues: 'When this distinction persists, *sola scriptura* becomes the seedbed of fundamentalism, as well as biblical criticism. It assumes that the text of the Scripture makes sense separate from a Church that gives it sense.'[86] Fundamentalism often confuses revelation with the Bible itself, which leads some to believe that anybody, anywhere can gain an accurate understanding of the text. This is misguided, for Hauerwas, because the only way to have a correct understanding of the Bible is to interpret it within the context of the ecclesial practices of the community that share a common history and categories of interpretation.[87]

If we attempt to make Scripture subject to apologetic justifications of truth, this is completely erroneous. For Hauerwas, rather than speaking to the *truth* of our beliefs as Christians, we should be demonstrating *truthfulness* in our lives by exhibiting Christian virtues in our faith communities.[88] Hauerwas offers a robust alternative to the rationalism found in principle ethics stemming from the influence of Kant. As with other postliberals, he is levelling a critique at the self-congratulatory pretentions of modernist liberalism that attempted to reduce ethics to correctly made rational decisions. This modernist presumption fails to recognize diversity of persons and cultures and assumes that human beings can make decisions with detached objectivity based on some universal notion of reason. Instead, ethics works subjectively, but within a community context. For Hauerwas, since the Enlightenment, philosophers have mistakenly attempted to make the notion of morality a universal concept. Instead, discussions of morality demand that we our attentive to our analogies, understanding that what constitutes moral development will vary from community to community.[89]

Again, it is important to note that Hauerwas' subjective ethic is by no means a private ethic that isolates the individual or forms an 'oppressive uniformity'. As Hauerwas wittily adds: 'Rather the mark of a truthful community is partly seen in how it enables the diversity of gifts and virtues to flourish. Therefore the church is not only a community of character but also a community of characters, since we are convinced that God rejoices in the diversity of spirits who inhabit his church.'[90] This is a community-focused virtue ethics. The liberal perspective of the world is that we have no story, so we are free to make our own story. Unfortunately, since we assume our stories are self-imposed, we become blind to aspects of coercion in the social orders in which we are situated, which prevents the habituation that is essential to maintain a virtuous life. But, as Christians, it is not that we create our own stories and make own ethical values. Instead, our stories are shaped by the Church community, which, in turn, shapes the individual. The Church provides the context for the moral education of its people through preaching, sharing, listening to others and participation in the liturgy as a community. This provides a sharp contrast to the radical, arrogant individualism of modernism and restores the Church to its central position as Christian community.[91]

Other voices in postliberal theology

There are many others we could mention who have offered insights and who may be considered influential in postliberal theological discussions. Unfortunately, due to space limitations and the focus of this book, we will limit ourselves to several key figures who, we believe, have made the most significant impact as principal sources in this movement. We will discuss each theologian in order of our estimation of his or her primary relevance to the development of postliberal theology.

David Kelsey (1932–)

As we mentioned before, Kelsey rightfully deserves a place in the origins or formation of what eventually became known as the 'Yale

School' of postliberal theology. Kelsey did his undergraduate and graduate work at Yale and has taught in the Yale Divinity School since 1965 where he is currently the Luther A. Weigle Professor of Theology Emeritus. In March 2011, Kelsey delivered the Warfield Lectures at Princeton Theological Seminary. Although Kelsey may be the less known of the 'big three' of the Yale School his influence as a colleague of both Lindbeck and Frei must not be downplayed.

Lindbeck claimed that doctrines were to be seen as the set of grammatical rules for the Christian community, rather than simply viewed as propositional truth claims. Frei claimed that the biblical narratives are not intended to lead us to historical facts. Kelsey's perspective is that our criteria of truth must be relevant for the discipline of inquiry. For example, the criteria of truth for the study of physics do not have the same relevance and applicability to that of history. And, the types of criterion that are deemed necessary for a particular field of inquiry are often governed and regulated internally by the given discipline itself. In fact, it may be logically possible, according to Kelsey, that certain authentic Christian beliefs or practices may be deemed false because the criteria for evaluating them as 'Christian' may be beyond the criteria whereby such things may be assessed.[92]

David Kelsey's book, *The Uses of Scripture in Modern Theology*, originally published in 1975,[93] most certainly had an influential hand in guiding postliberal theology. Although Kelsey was younger than Hans Frei, his thinking challenged Frei's and Lindbeck's own theological development.[94] Paul J. DeHart claims that the way in which Kelsey's book was received by Frei and Lindbeck 'made it something of a catalyst for what later emerged as postliberalism'. Furthermore, DeHart continues, Kelsey's work not only helped 'to move Hans Frei closer to Lindbeck in emphasizing theological interpretation of the Bible as an inevitably communal and tradition-shaped practice (as opposed to the mere decipherment of meanings objectively given as a function of literary structure)' but it also helped focus 'Lindbeck's attention to the question of 'textuality' and thus moved him in his turn closer to Frei and, in particular, to Frei's interpretation of Karl Barth.'[95]

Kelsey provides three major points with regard to the question as to what makes a certain text or texts deemed as 'Christian scripture' to the church. First, a text is called 'Christian scripture' if it functions in particular ways in the church; that is, by what is does in the church by what it expresses, renders, occasions or proposes when it is used in a particular manner. Second, a text is considered 'Christian scripture' if it is used to transform a person's life and shape one's character. When a text is used to lead one to salvation, providing a change of belief and redemption of the person, this is a clear characteristic of 'Christian scripture'. The third point Kelsey emphasizes as to what determines whether a text is taken as 'Christian scripture' is that it will be used in the life of a Christian community for the identity of individuals within that community. In summary, scriptural authority is not about the description of the properties of the texts, but about how the texts are used in various ways 'for the common life of the Christian community'.[96] The texts do not hold some independent qualities that accord them the status of 'scripture' and hence declare them 'authoritative'. Instead, they are given their authoritative status of 'scripture' primarily because of their use in and functions for the life and community of the church. One's interpretive context is critical for how one interprets the patterns in the biblical narratives. The texts designated as 'scripture' are then used normatively in doing theology. The community adopts certain rules that govern how theology is to be done. So scripture is authoritative not on the basis of the text itself, but on the basis of how the text is recognized in the ecclesial community.[97]

Kelsey illustrates this with a parable about a group of boys on an empty lot with a soft rubber ball. One boy says: 'Let's play ball' and the group divides into teams. An outside, unknowing observer would not know at this point what game the boys were about to play; it could be basketball, soccer, football or something else. However, the observer assumes that the game will in some way involve doing something with the ball according to a previously agreed or assumed set of rules. Somewhat instinctively, based on the location of their meeting and/or other presupposed factors, the boys will all understand which game they are about to play with the ball. In a similar fashion, Kelsey points out, when a theologian submits that scripture is the authority for the practice of theology or for this or that theological proposal, he or she is committed to a certain agreed set of activities or agreed rules that govern such activity.[98] Previous acceptance and common practice determine the authoritative qualifications for the community.

But simply due to a common understanding and acceptance of the general rules in the community context is not to say that there are no differences in how specific tasks ought to be done. Kelsey elucidates this in the following:

> When a particular theologian says, 'Scripture is the authority for this theological proposal,' he is not making a descriptive claim about scripture, nor is he committing himself to an entire family of activities as such. Rather he is committing himself to a particular understanding of theology's task. And just as in our parable the boys' decision about which ball game to play determined just how they construe the ball and what they do with it, so a theologian's decision about what the task or point is of 'doing theology' determines how he will construe scripture and by what rules he will use it so as to authorize his own theological proposals.[99]

Several theologians may have a common commitment to a certain set of practices and 'rules' of faith, but still approach specific theological tasks differently and hold a variety of theological commitments with regard to particular issues.

William Placher rightly points out similarities between Kelsey's call for the use of scripture in Christian community and the challenge posed by Stanley Hauerwas we mentioned earlier. It is the Bible being used within the common life and community of the Church that both shapes and influences the identity of the people within the community. David Lauber claims that Kelsey's unique contribution to postliberal theology moves beyond the more typical descriptive or functional analysis provided by Lindbeck, to a more prescriptive proposal as to *why* scripture should be used in the context of the church community. Lauber claims this contribution of Kelsey is often overlooked. God uses the Church and her use of scripture for the formation of both the identity of the community and the individual within the community through the Holy Spirit. In this regard, bibliology is situated within theology proper.[100]

We would suggest that the converse of this is also true: God uses the community and the individual within the community to form the identity of the Church and her use of scripture within that community. Kelsey himself affirms this dialectical relationship between the Christian scripture and the Christian church. The various activities of the Church, that is, practices of the Church as they are arranged to reach various ends, define the Church.

The Church's faithfulness to these practices depends on God's presence in the Church, and the Church's use of written texts as 'scripture' for ongoing guidance and reformation. In order for the Church to *be* 'Church' it demands certain uses of its scripture in which God's presence is revealed. These texts, as scripture, will be used in a regulative matter for the behaviour of the Church community.[101] As Kelsey puts it: 'Just as some concepts such as "Christian church" are defined in terms of "Christian scripture", so the concept "Christian scripture" is defined in terms of some concepts "Christian church".'[102] God formed the community, and the community formed, under the guidance (and authorship) of the Holy Spirit, the Church and its scriptures. In turn, the scriptures formed within this Holy Spirit-led community, continue to form the identity of that community. Scripture and Church community exist in constant dialectic and in continual reliance on one another. In other words, scripture forms the Church, and the Church forms the scriptures – all under the direction and guidance of the Holy Spirit. Kelsey's prescriptive proposal is extremely relevant, because awareness of this interdependent relationship between scripture and community shows why scripture must be used in the Church, but it also shows why the Church must be viewed in the context of the scriptures.

William Placher (1948–2008)

William Placher was a the LaFollette Distinguished Professor in the Humanities and Chair of the Department of Philosophy and Religion at Wabash College in Crawfordsville, Indiana, prior to his death in 2008. Placher also may be considered to be a part of the 'Yale School' context of postliberal theology. Following his study of philosophy and religion as an undergraduate at Wabash College, he attended Yale Divinity school, where he studied under Hans Frei. Placher, a devout Presbyterian, was known for his charitable scholarship, clear writing and excellence in teaching. He was a gifted communicator, and was straightforward on his association with postliberal theology, readily observed in such books as *Unapologetic Theology: A Christian Voice in a Pluralistic Conversation* (1989) and later, *The Triune God: An Essay in Postliberal Theology* (2007).

Placher provides his own nuanced history with respect to postliberal theology most succinctly perhaps in an article he wrote titled, 'Being Postliberal: A Response to James Gustafson'. Placher submits that when he was a graduate student in theology in the early 1970s that Bultmannian studies were commonplace among New Testament scholars. During this time, Hans Frei was demanding more attention to the narratives of the Bible while claiming we should think less about historical, cultural contexts. Frei (as we have seen) challenged us to begin with the biblical narratives themselves rather than with a modern philosophical framework to which the narratives must fit in order to be culturally relevant. Placher was strongly influenced by these demands, along with Frei's encouragement to read Barth, of whom few students were reading at the time due to the dominant influence of Bultmann.[103] Placher followed Frei in moving the emphasis away from the individual's experience of the text in terms of existential relevance, back to the narrative of the text itself.

But where Frei stressed the unity of the biblical narrative and its internal coherence, Placher rather emphasized the plurality of narratives in the Bible. There are various stories about Jesus in the Gospel narratives and also many genres other than straightforward historical accounts. In all cases, one reads the Bible seriously, but it takes additional work to understand these various layers of truth. One must affirm the truth of the Bible while continuing to struggle with its meaning. For example, in the parable of the Good Samaritan, nobody is concerned about whether or not the injured man on the road or the Samaritan are historical figures. We understand this narrative as a parable, so the truth of the narrative is conveyed within this understanding. Nevertheless, 'true' is always true at all times and in all cultures, but the way by which truth is argued (or not argued) will vary depending on the conversation partner.[104] Placher helps us see that looking to genres as well as cultural backgrounds and assumptions are not reasons for an easy dismissal of biblical truth, but just the opposite. We must discover the context in which truth is conveyed without first assuming all narrative is structured in a literal, historical framework.

As Placher also argued in *Unapologetic Theology*, he believes that truth is universal, but the manner by which we defend a claim of truth is always contextual and conditioned by one's culture and traditions. Although he does not deny the need for ad hoc apologetics, for Placher, postliberal theology is not primarily about apologetics, historical arguments or scientific facts that have been characteristic interests of more mainstream evangelicals. In Placher's view, some strands of evangelicalism that harbour on such modernist tendencies seem more akin to philosophical positivism and empiricism or to the Republican right than they are to an authentic Christian tradition.[105] Placher's reflections on these matters point us to a question that is characteristically postliberal. The postliberal theologian consistently (or faithfully we should say perhaps) asks: Why should systems of knowledge and fact finding based on suppositions outside our faith context be allowed to set the terms for our dialogue and understanding as Christians?

Placher claims that 'his project' is 'to connect a radical view of God's transcendence with a narrative Christology' through a robust doctrine of the Holy Spirit, which he elucidates in his book, *The Triune God*.[106] In this work, Placher submits that a Christian is not one who proves the existence of God, but is one who recognizes and confesses the Jesus of the Gospels as Lord, the self-revealing word made flesh. This 'epistemology' however, stems not from the intellectual rigours of foundationalism, but through what he calls an 'epistemology of the Spirit'. The way we come to know is through personal transformation through appropriate religious practice by the grace of God's Holy Spirit in and through the community of Jesus' followers throughout history. For Placher, the epistemology of the Spirit is not a flattening of the Spirit's work into pure cognition, but it refers to our faith as human beings as we embrace both head and heart. Divisions between the intellect and affections are inappropriate and simply incorrect. Of course, bemoaning such artificial bifurcations is nothing new to postliberal theology, as suspicions of such divisions have been seen in the work of Augustine up through Calvin and Jonathan Edwards.[107] Postliberal theology is simply bringing them to the fore once again.

Placher also draws on Moltmann to help articulate how the Trinity helps us with a postliberal perspective of community and relationality with the story of Jesus. The Trinity is a model of equality with difference; mutuality with functional diversity among persons, persons not has isolated individuals (an abuse of modernism), but persons within community. The story of Jesus is found within Jesus' position in the Trinity. Equality and mutuality, as with the Trinity, is nothing that is ever transcended

or superseded for the sake of individual rights or power.[108] We
can see how Placher's postliberal theology is distinctly expressed
in both his denials and affirmations. He denies the disunity in
heart and mind that he believes stems from a misplaced dualism
of modernist thought. We are living creatures, not simply cognitive
beings; persons who are created for community in the image of the
God who created us. We live in a community of faith tied to the
life of Jesus and his followers throughout history and revealed to
us through the Holy Spirit in and through that broad community.
Jesus is identified within the Trinity of the Godhead, in mutual
communion with the Father and the Holy Spirit – a model of the
unity and diversity we are to share with others.

With this in mind, it is no wonder why it has been said
that Placher's metaphor for doing theology is conversation.
Conversation allows its participants to maintain perspectives and
hold beliefs. A postliberal theology navigates between the self-
descriptive efforts of a Christian community and conversational
engagement with those outside the community. Of course, it is
impossible to remain a community without common beliefs and
convictions at some level. It is not the case that a commitment to
conversation requires the suspension of committed beliefs in favour
of some notion of objective neutrality.[109] In fact, we could argue
that it is the commitments and beliefs (along with the practices
that follow) that provide the impetus for productive and engaging
conversation. If beliefs and convictions were simply abandoned
for the pursuit of neutral ground, would conversation even be
meaningful or required?

This emphasis is important for the future of postliberal theology,
because it must not be reduced to a mere theology of description or
grammar. First of all, it cannot be reduced to the task of description
and remain intellectually honest. Theology always involves
perspectives, backgrounds, cultural frameworks and ecclesiological
contexts. These are here to stay, regardless of any attempt to put
them aside in search of some ever-elusive neutrality. In fact, the
belief that one must seek neutrality in theology, and the means
by which one goes about seeking such presupposed neutrality,
also betray a certain theological perspective. Second, theological
convictions are essential for the practice and maintenance of the
community and for the transformative tasks it seeks to accomplish
for those outside the community of faith. We believe that William

Placher's work makes a helpful contribution to postliberal theology by keeping this conviction–conversation element of the community in order.

Bruce D. Marshall (1955–)

Bruce D. Marshall, Lehman professor of Christian Doctrine at Southern Methodist University's Perkins School of Theology, is another postliberal theologian also drawing on an epistemology of the Spirit and looking toward a model of the Trinity to distinguish a unity of truth within the Christian community.

As we will note more specifically in the next chapter, the subject of truth has often been a key criticism of those proposing a postliberal model of theology. Marshall addresses this concern straightforwardly in his book, *Trinity and Truth*. Marshall, drawing heavily on Aquinas and the analytic philosopher Donald Davidson, also acknowledges the influence of both Frei and Lindbeck in his postliberal treatise for a trinitarian understanding of truth. For Marshall, Christians do not need to borrow notions of truth that are foreign to a Christian way of belief and practice, but they need to understand their distinctiveness as a religious community centred in the triune God.[110] By no means does Marshall shirk a philosophically robust analysis of the nature of truth, as some purporting a narrative approach to theology have been accused, but he provides a detailed analysis for a trinitarian postliberal epistemic justification.

Marshall points out that both communities and individuals differ as to what constitutes truth and what it takes to call something 'true'. One set of arguments may be convincing for some, but not for others. Deciding on how to adjudicate between positions of truth and justification is a standard problem among philosophers.[111] With the philosopher Donald Davidson, Marshall borrows from an anti-foundational analytic philosophical perspective to shape his reflections on a trinitarian understanding of truth. Our beliefs in what is true are not justified by some ultimate foundational belief that serves as a fulcrum for other beliefs, but instead they are justified as they cohere with our other beliefs in the Christian community. With Lindbeck and contra Schleiermacher, Marshall would affirm that experience is dependent on our beliefs; it does not ground our beliefs.[112] Applied to his trinitarian proposal of truth, Marshall states:

> If a community holds true the identification of God as Father, Son and Holy Spirit only insofar as that identification fails to conflict with some other beliefs, then those other beliefs, not the trinitarian identification, will be the ones this community is least willing to give up. ... the Christian community will have to decide that its own most central beliefs are true by recognizing that their centrality presumes their epistemic primacy; it presumes of them the distinctive status of those beliefs with which others must fit in order to be true.[113]

It is not that these beliefs must seek outside help in order to be justified as true and worthy, instead, the justification is made internally, within the distinctive context of the Christian community. However, it is from the Father and the Incarnate Son, but *through* the Holy Spirit, by which we are convicted of the truth of the central teachings of Christian community. This does not guarantee that the specific beliefs that we hold are in fact true, because many 'competing' truth claims may still be consistent with our primary Christian beliefs. The Spirit provides us with the conviction that our primary, central beliefs of the Church are true and then teaches us to 'order the rest of our beliefs accordingly'. The Spirit's job then, is to make sure that our beliefs are generally true in accord with the central convictions of the Christian community.[114] Marshall is saying that it is not simply about our pursuit of truth and belief, but it is ultimately God's activity through the Spirit by which we are granted access to truth and belief.

Is this mere fideism? Marshall contends that it is not. In order to be epistemically responsible we often mistakenly believe that we must hold all beliefs by the same rational standards. If beliefs do not have justifiable reasons that 'everyone' holds true, then we may be charged with fideism. But this is not the way that anyone comes to ultimately believe anything. Reasons for beliefs can only go so far, before our beliefs simply appeal to a 'nexus of belief' that we, along with our dialogue partners, simply hold true *without* giving reasons (epistemically primary beliefs). Marshall suggests that to hold beliefs rationally means that we have the wisdom to discern between when we need or need not give reasons for our beliefs. If we needed to provide reasons for all our beliefs all the time, then we would all be fideistic, because it simply could not be done. In this manner, Marshall believes that the charge of fideism is 'self-refuting'. He is nonetheless careful on this point. Simply because we are not required to give reasons for each of our beliefs does not imply that we simply choose at will which of our beliefs require reasons. Also, we must be willing to change a particular belief if sufficient reasons are given to do so. However, simply because we may be able to provide conditions under which we may have to abandon certain beliefs, this does not mean that we actually will ever need to abandon certain beliefs. In fact, we should continue to hold our most basic beliefs with certainty in the Church community, being confident that the conditions for disbelief will never arise.[115]

Granted, much more would need to be said if we were to discuss Marshall's entire argument throughout his book. Nonetheless, with Marshall's rigorous application of philosophy, his primary focus is clear: It is ultimately the triune God, through the Spirit who provides the conviction of the truth of beliefs to the church community.[116] We must not conflate our epistemic priorities with assumed priorities imposed on us by rationalism. For Marshall, it is indeed possible to be postliberal and post-rationalistic without abandoning epistemic justification. We may have epistemic rational integrity beyond mere rationalism, as we maintain our epistemic priorities and beliefs common to the Christian faith community.

George Hunsinger

The renowned Barthian scholar, George Hunsinger[117] is a postliberal theologian who is also known as a significant interpreter of Hans Frei. Hunsinger, also a Presbyterian, teaches at Princeton Theological Seminary, where he is the Hazel Thompson McCord Professor of Systematic Theology.

Hunsinger wrote an article to Hans Frei, for Frei's 65th birthday, which describes what Hunsinger calls 'a sympathetic reworking of the Lindbeck typology to direct it more plausibly along postliberal lines'.[118] Hunsinger accomplishes this reworking through the eyes of Barth. Hunsinger contends that Barth transcends the competing options of literalism (which Lindbeck calls cognitive

propositionalism) and expressivism (emotional expressivism per
Lindbeck). Barth's approach is rather a 'hermeneutical realism'.
An example of this perspective is found in Barth's rendering of the
empty tomb. For Barth, the literal, objective status of the empty
tomb apart from the scriptural narrative is not nearly as important
as our affirmation of the living Christ. The truth to which the
Resurrection refers is precisely this point: Jesus lives! The Jesus
who incarnated as the word of God, who lived among us, died,
was buried and put into a tomb, is the Jesus who is alive and
was made manifest in body and soul. Rather than emphasizing
the empty tomb as a factual event to be proved with apologetics,
Barth focuses on the risen Christ.[119] We can readily see the parallels
with and the importance of Barth (via Hunsinger at this point)
with respect to other postliberal perspectives. If we focus on the
factuality of the events rather than the narrative of the Bible itself,
then we may easily misplace our efforts by attempting to satisfy the
demands of facticity imposed from without, while neglecting the
truth from within.

But Barth did not accept an expressivist interpretation of
scripture either, that rendered the texts as mere metaphorical or
emotional responses to meaningful religious occurrences. However,
the metaphors and imaginative images used in the Bible were no
less true, even if they could not submit to the stringent requirements of literalism. If God is described with wings, having a face
or being angry, then these metaphors must never lose their full
semantic force. Simply because we are not required to take such
terms literally, does not mean that they should be morphed into
simple emotional or symbolic abstractions for our comprehension.
For Barth, in fact all our descriptions of God are essentially
anthropomorphic renderings. Our concepts and language and
understandings are all human, so all communication about God
will be coloured and shaped by this inescapable situatedness.
For the expressivist, the way we select our metaphors in order
to meaningfully speak about God results from our emotional
experiences and personal needs. So, our metaphors will change,
based on our needs at a specific time, place or culture. For Barth
however, the metaphors used in the Bible are not flexible, but fixed
according to the revelation of God through analogy. Since God
chose, through His word, his own 'self-analogization,' then by His
grace the metaphors used truly correspond to God Himself – even

when they are portrayed under a culturally conditioned humanity. If scripture refers to God's 'arm' or 'mouth', then, by analogy, these images primarily refer to God acting and speaking, rather than to human body parts. The metaphors have their truth first in God, and only secondarily in creation.[120] Ultimately then, what is in the narrative, must remain in the narrative. God chose how he wanted to communicate Himself, so God chose how best to do this. Since God chose the metaphors, we should protect them.

Hunsinger effectively points out that Barth's emphasis on this analogical relationship between the text and the referent demonstrates his opposition to the univocal, literalist approach to interpretation that fails to rightfully address God's mystery within the context of revelation. It also shows his distaste for the equivocal approach of the expressivists that fails to rightfully address the clarity of God's revelation in scripture. God is sovereign and He can reveal Himself as he so chooses by whatever means he chooses to address us. For Barth, the alternative lies in looking at our references to God analogically. This honours both God's mystery and ineffability and the perspicuity of scripture with those who are personally addressed by God with both head and heart.[121]

Hunsinger points out that Barth's proposals here both converge and diverge from Lindbeck's, *The Nature of Doctrine*. Lindbeck, like Barth, claims that doctrinal truths are both 'intrasystemic' and 'performative'. They are fully self-involving and committed to a particular way of thinking inherent to the nature of the doctrines themselves. Barth however, does not imply that the referential truth of doctrines is dependent on existential Christian practice, as Lindbeck seems to imply. For Barth, doctrinal truths are doctrinal truths regardless of their performance. Likewise, Hunsinger submits that our lives develop in response to truthful propositions, but the propositions themselves are true independent from our actions on them.[122]

Regardless of this difference, these points still show the larger picture of Barth's theological understanding and influence on postliberal theology. Barth did not attempt to make theology fit within modernist demands for neutral, universally established truth or foundations for the assertions of truth. In fact, he did just the opposite. Theological truth is not universally accessible at all, neither is it self-evident. It is rather a contextually based, and subjectively involved understanding. God reveals theological truth, and it makes no difference whether or not it is anthropologically relevant. Barth is not denying all aspects of theological justification, but justification is determined on the basis of correspondence with scripture, rather than correspondence with external and imposed notions of universal criteria.[123] Hunsinger's appropriation of Barth reminds us again of significant features of Barth's contributions to the formation of postliberal theology and its unswerving commitment to narrative *as* narrative.

Kathryn Tanner

Kathryn Tanner, another professor at Yale, is an additional (yet critical) voice on the postliberal theological scene. Tanner completed her undergraduate and graduate education at Yale prior to her teaching post in systematic theology at Chicago Divinity School where she taught for 16 years. In 2010 she joined the faculty of Yale Divinity School, where she is currently the Frederick Marquand Professor of Systematic Theology.

As we noted with William Placher, our unity comes from our identity with Jesus and his followers throughout history, through an 'epistemology of the Spirit'. Our unity with diversity is modelled in the triune God. Both William Placher and Bruce Marshall emphasized an epistemology of the Spirit, looking to the Trinity for insights on a postliberal commitment to community with unity and diversity. Kathryn Tanner also strongly emphasizes diversity with unity in her version of postliberal theology. With Tanner, unity comes not through exactness on beliefs and practices, but on a common commitment to pursue Christian practices of discipleship from the life of Jesus.

In one of her earlier works, *Theories of Culture: A New Agenda for Theology*, she begins with a tracing of the background behind how the English word 'culture' takes on an anthropological sense in various contexts and cultures. Tanner submits that the modern anthropological approach to culture that embraces difference and diversity of beliefs and values with 'a disinterested suspension of judgment' in order to provide a more fair description or under-standing of a particular culture, has come under severe criticism in postmodern cultural anthropology. The myth of disinterested, de-historicized cultural objectivity has been clearly disclosed.

Tanner draws from postmodern theory to emphasize that cultures are not defined in terms of their consensus based norms; they are dynamic, hybrid and constantly interactive. Modern theology's mistake was viewing culture in a manner that was too restrictive and self-contained. Tanner separates from Lindbeckian postliberalism on this point with its selective following of Wittgenstein. Lindbeck draws from Wittgenstein to develop a rule or grammatical approach to Christian faith, but neglects the applicational problems to fixed communal practices that stem from such rule following.[124] This other side of the coin from the 'grammar' and 'rules' is not adequately considered, according to Tanner.

For Tanner, culture is produced, and is also *being* produced. It is not simply some entity or discipline that may be evaluated apart from a particular historical context. Christian theology itself is culturally produced and shaped by specific Christian social practices. Theology has been mistakenly associated with an intellectual discipline of the academic elite, with writings produced for dialogue with others in the same ivory towers. As a highly specialized field, it is often seen as insignificant to the everyday concerns of many. However, this should not be so. Christian theology as a culture must not be considered the same as what is commonly referred to as 'high culture' literature and philosophical writings. Instead, Christian theology is about Christian practices in society in everyday life.[125] As Tanner submits:

> Christian theology in this primary sense would, accordingly, be found embedded in such matters as the way altar and pews are arranged. Their placement usually has a meaning, a theological aspect, in that it embodies a sense of the difference between minister and laity, and between God and human beings. All Christian activities would have a meaning or theological dimension in this sense—going to church, protesting poverty, praying, and helping one's neighbor. They are socially significant Christian actions in virtue of being constituted by a sense of what Christians believe and how they should lead their lives.[126]

We recall how David Kelsey spoke about boys playing ball with a set of rules as a parallel to theologians putting scripture forward as the rulebook authority for the practice of theology. When the 'rules' have been presupposed and agreed in advance, then the theologian is committed to the rules that govern the practices of the discipline.[127] But what are we to think of Christians who have not been trained to play properly? What if simply having the rules of the game does not lead to agreement among those with various backgrounds?

The rules and presuppositions seem to be less restrictive for Tanner than those to which Kelsey referred. Kelsey seemed to clearly state that if the presupposed assumptions to 'play ball' implied the game was to be baseball, then bouncing the ball would be out of the question. For Tanner, however, rather than dismissing those with whom we disagree as being uninformed or improperly trained, it is more charitable to come to grips with the fact that even Christians trained in the 'rules' do not necessarily come to complete agreement. The 'rules of the game do not keep Christians who want to bounce the ball out of a game in which others bat it; the identity of the Christian game is not that restrictive.' Nonetheless, Tanner is careful to say that such inclusive perspective does not imply equal judgements about the propriety of those playing the game. But it does mean that 'the propriety of their respective judgments will have to be determined in the course of playing the game.' What happens, then if the rules do not determine agreement? Tanner claims that this demonstrates that simply referring to the rules of the game does not necessarily determine its right practice. Arguments other than rulebook arguments, such as those that support specific Christian practices in the course of game must be provided to make a determination of their propriety.[128]

For Tanner, there is nothing internal to Christian social practices themselves that unites Christian practice or some common demand for social conformity of common demands. Christians are agreed that Christian beliefs and practices certainly do witness to the God of whom they are disciples. In saying this, however, it is not to say that all Christians agree on precisely *which* beliefs and practices provide this witness. So the unity does not come from agreement on some shared particular beliefs or specific practices but rather on the common commitment to keep pursuing those practices that do, in effect, characterize true discipleship. In other words, they have 'a shared sense of the importance of figuring it out'. Although Tanner does emphasize that 'Scriptures, the creeds, the eucharist, and baptism are places where Christian believe the Word of God is heard, where the Word of God is present.' Additionally, she acknowledges that the significance of Jesus' life and practices are critical to how the Christian is to live.[129] This diversified unity is crucial for the Christian because we are fallible as humans and need correction from others. Diversity provides us with a strong reminder that we cannot control the free acts and movements of God and His word.[130]

It may be apparent that Tanner is not in favour of claims for the exclusivity or superiority of the truth of Christianity. Instead of making exclusive truth claims, Christians should be offering a way of life of discipleship following Christ. But this life of discipleship will be represented by rich diversity and constant change within Christianity. Gary Dorrien believes that Tanner's revised version of postliberal theology places her actually closer to the classic theological liberalism of Albrecht Ritschl that it does to Karl Barth. Barth's emphasis on revelation from God is substituted with the inspiration of communities of faith.[131] For Barth, it was the theological that revealed the anthropological. For Tanner, it is the anthropological that reveals the theological.

Ronald Theimann, James W. McClendon Jr and John Milbank

As we conclude this more or less encyclopedic rendering of 'other voices' in the postliberal theological movement, due to space and scope, we will give cursory mention to three more influential figures. However, we must leave the harvesting of the resources they offer to the future research of our readers.

Ronald Thiemann (also a graduate of Yale) is a Lutheran theologian who has also been identified with postliberal theology. He submits that revelation must be understood as the 'narrated promise' of God. It is God who prevenes all speech and actions. Theology presupposes the prevenience of God's initiative and activity. Revelation then is not epistemologically linked to foundationalism, as many have mistakenly presumed, but to the narrative of scripture that disclosed the God who promises. Revelation guards this basic Christian conviction of God's prevenience, so in this sense it is part of theology proper.[132]

Adonis Vidu identifies James W. McClendon Jr as a postliberal theologian who is often neglected. Even back in 1975, McClendon was interacting with speech act theory in J. L. Austin and John Searle. For McClendon, it is the linguistic community and its social practices that provide stability of meaning in our communication. There is a triad, a holistic 'web', consisting of speech, knowledge and practice. Speech is not something distinct from action, but it is a form of performative action that arises from certain conventions. Thus, meaning actually arises from the background of practice. But McClendon does not merely dismiss the notion of truth as a matter of contextual suitability, only available within a particular community. We need correctives. McClendon's proposal is quite simple: maintain a practice of Bible reading. Of course his proposal must still address why we recognize scripture as scripture and reflect on interpretive conventions for reading scripture that presuppose the provision of meaning to one degree or the other.[133]

The esteemed, prolific theologian John Milbank's 'Radical Orthodoxy' arguably presents another 'brand' or version of postliberal theology. Like others, Milbank finds our Christian knowledge within our own context in the community of the Church, not in some external validation by the social sciences or elsewhere. Christian theology must not succumb to the knowledge demands of 'outsider' disciplines that adhere to a completely different set of narratives, standards and claims. If it were to do so, then it would be denying its own essential standards of theological truth. The most fundamental event that interprets all other events is the 'interruption' of Christ and His bride, the Church. Theology is to continue this narrative among the community of faith.[134] But rather than arguing, as Bruce Marshall does, for an analytically robust trinitarian proposal on the nature of truth, Milbank and one of his postliberal theological protégées, Catherine Pickstock, developed a liturgical perspective on truth – it is in the Eucharistic event where we meet the truth of God.[135]

We have certainly neglected to mention some authors who would prefer to be identified as postliberal or those who have indeed contributed to the development of postliberal theology. Others we have identified may prefer, no doubt, not to embrace the label 'postliberal', but they nevertheless seemed to fit the broad strokes we have attempted to paint that would often characterize a postliberal theology. In spite of our own limitations and oversights, we trust these few examples have helped in providing an introductory perspective on this rich theological movement.

CHAPTER 4

Problems and criticisms of postliberalism

In suggesting that there are problems and criticisms of 'postliberal theology', it naturally assumes that there is some cohesive understanding of such a movement. Granted, we believe such an assumption is fair. But it would be mistaken to take from this assumption that this necessarily implies that postliberal theology is a monolithic theological system. After our investigations thus far, if there is one thing we realize among postliberal theologians it is the reluctance and aversion to systematization. Postliberal theology, whatever it is, cannot be divorced from narrative and cannot be disengaged from the narratives of these respective theologians we have mentioned. This is not to say that we are unable to isolate various themes provided by these theologians in order to bring to light several noted problems with a postliberal turn in theology. In order to do this, we will first consider three major overarching criticisms: the question of truth, the issue of apologetics and religious diversity and the problem of relating to contemporary culture. Several more specific criticisms will be subsumed under these three major criticisms for heuristic purposes.

The question of truth

It is evident that postliberal theology emphasizes the cultural–linguistic and intratextual aspects of doctrine, while at the same time de-emphasizing both the theologically liberal emphasis on human experience and the conservative emphasis on propositional truth claims. Consequently, it is often criticized for proposing a denial of absolute truth and hence promoting relativism.[1] Postliberal theologians are accused of reducing truth to that which accords faithfulness in life and church community to the narrative of scripture. This being the case, some believe this is sacrificing the entire notion of truth. But does this not simply beg the entire question of truth? If the church community is faithfully applying the narrative of scripture, does this not presuppose an understanding of that narrative and the ability of the community to interpret that narrative?[2] In order for constructive dialogue to occur on this issue, it is important to realize that it is not truth that is denied or devalued in postliberal theology, it is the question of how truth is obtained and what we promote and define as 'truth'. If truth simply means that which is verified by supposed universal standards of verification within a rationalistic or empirical paradigm of knowledge, then the postliberal theologian would certainly deny the need for her theological understanding to succumb to such an 'outside' justification. In fact, putting theology to such a test would in fact be denying the very truth of that theology which the postliberal is affirming. The *via crucis* and the community of Jesus is not obliged to adapt the *via scientia*. This is not to say that science and religion are in conflict, but it is to say that the language and scientific method must not be imposed on the way of faith, and vice versa.

Certainly, postliberal theology encourages a pragmatic approach to 'truth' as it pertains to both scripture and tradition applied to the Church community. Truth is practice within community, not merely logical or empirical propositions imposed on the community from outside. However, simply because postliberal theologians emphasize a practice centred understanding of truth, does not *de facto* imply that it excludes ontological or metaphysical commitments.[3] The metaphysical realist claims that there is indeed a world 'out there' that is external or independent of my own perceptions or cognitive experiences. The postliberal is often understood to be promoting a metaphysical antirealism that denies a reality that is external to the minds of its perceivers. The metaphysical antirealist would suggest that the reality of objects such as toothbrushes, automobiles, and the moon is completely dependent on human perception. Conflating this perception of metaphysical antirealism with postliberal theology rests on a misunderstanding and misreading of its project and purpose.[4]

Jeffrey Hensley points out two major variations of metaphysical antirealism that will help us understand why this misunderstanding may occur for those critiquing the postliberal theological project. First, there is a *conceptual* antirealism that would not deny the literal existence of material objects, but would segment objects into conceptual schemes and create an interrelationship between objects and our experiences for our overall understanding of reality. Again, it is not that 'real' objects do not exist (as with metaphysical idealism) but they are not understandable and classifiable according to a perspective of 'existence' unless we apply our concepts of understanding to our experience. The second sort of metaphysical antirealism, known as *alethic* antirealism, claims that truth is always dependent on cognitive constructions and representations of experience. There is no neutral way by which we can escape our own concepts of understanding. So truth, by nature, is an internal agreement among propositions and beliefs, rather than some sort of accord with propositions and beliefs external to the human mind.[5] Hensely argues, however, that George Lindbeck's postliberal theology takes *neither* variation of antirealism, but rather points to antifoundationalism. When Lindbeck submits that our experiences of reality are concept laden, he is not denying an external reality or affirming a conceptual antirealism. Rather, he is stating that we use concepts as humans to both understand our experiences and describe them to others.[6]

Unfortunately, the postliberal rejection of classic Cartesian foundationalism is often characterized as the slippery slope toward relativism and the absence of truth altogether. But this is surely mistaken. We must not confuse an explanation of the means by which we come to knowledge (epistemology) of our faith, with that which we embrace *as* knowledge. Postliberals such as George Lindbeck, of course, are not attempting to work out a full-scale epistemology, but are rather speaking to the nature of our Christian understanding of faith and doctrine. Again, postliberals are not denying the notion of truth, but they are affirming an understanding of truth that moves beyond the reduction of truth to empirical correspondence. The postliberal certainly affirms truth, but it is a truth that points to an internal coherence within the

Christian narrative practiced in Christian community, rather than that which is ascribed to something that appears to find accord with a metaphysical foundation. Truth is not simply about representation lying on the surface of an empirical verificationist theory of meaning. It is unfortunate that the looming temptation to reduce truth in this manner can ultimately silence the voice of religion.[7] But postliberal theologians will not allow this silence, because they will not accept the modernist paradigm that carries the muzzle.

Bruce Marshall's distinction between alethiology and epistemology regarding truth is instructive at this juncture. Alethiology is about the meaning of claiming a proposition is true and epistemology is about how humans know and justify that which is classified as 'true'. George Lindbeck holds to a realist alethiology and a coherentist, pragmatic epistemology. This stems from his belief that God is the standard for truth, and that human understanding is always finite and in process. It is not that our expressed propositional statements of truth do not refer to a reality external to our minds, but we cannot ultimately test the full accuracy of such truth claims since we lack a 'God's eye' view on reality.[8] With this in mind, it is important not to represent postliberal theology as a movement that simply dismisses truth or does not take the issue of truth seriously. Neither is it the case that it is only philosophically minded postliberal theologians such as Bruce Marshall, who grapple with the subject of truth. This is simply wrongheaded. Rather, postliberal theology is affirming a particular expression of truth that moves beyond the reduction of truth to a cognitive–propositional approach.

A particular theory of truth and certainty that is derived from modernism, that operates independent of the gospel, may distort the 'internal mysteries and certainties' of the gospel. A modernist approach to certainty must be 'leavened by a more modest view that allows for an ineffaceable degree of subjectivity, commitment, cultural–historical location and other forms of self-involvement in all our cognitive judgments, then fact and meaning, cognition and performance, mystery and clarity' so that 'humility and certainty need no longer be so radically divorced from one another as they are by the epistemological excesses of modernity.'[9]

By definition, postliberal theology is moving beyond modernist reductions of truth of linguistic or historical positivism (truth as one-to-one correspondence between propositions and references) to a more relational or communal understanding of truth. This does not have as much to do with whether some*thing*, person or state of affairs exists or occurs in reality, but rather the means by which we come to understand or describe things, persons or historical events. All our descriptions of reality are always mediated in and through our embedded participation in particular contexts and communities. There is no unbiased, neutral means by which we can otherwise describe reality. In a manner of speaking, truth cannot be meaningfully explained apart from our descriptions of truth that are always mediated. We must be careful not to confuse the means by which we obtain (to whatever imperfect level or degree) an understanding of truth to the nature of truth itself. Another way of putting it would be thus: the way we come to know what we claim as 'truth' is different than that which we classify as 'truth'. For example, if truth only pertains to logical propositions, then you could not meaningfully speak of the emotions you feel for your family as 'truth'. For postliberal theology, truth does not refer to truth statements or propositions (which always refer to something beyond themselves as signifiers), but refers to the person of Jesus, the story of the gospel narratives and our participation within those narratives as a church community today.

This more full-orbed presentation of truth is also described by D. Stephen Long as he refers to Charles Taylor's work in this regard. Taylor looks to a tradition of truth rendering from Kant to Wittgenstein that rejects representationalism (sentences justified on the basis of other sentences) and draws on transcendental arguments. Long applies Taylor's insights to the incarnation of Jesus, the living truth of God. In this, truth, love, reason, and will, are all brought together in unity. Wittgenstein's work helped to dethrone philosophy from its privileged seat by exposing its limitations. His work is by no means rejecting truth, but provides a reframing of truth that is engaged, as with the virtue of love, rather than detached as a pure rationality. It is not that love and truth are opposites, for both are essential for complete knowledge. Truth is about participation and engagement, not detached objectivity. If truth is merely reduced to propositions that correspond with other propositions, then we are misguided. As Christians, we must realize that it is more about the 'who' than it is about the 'what'. Truth is more than written dogma alone; it is the practice of that dogma found in the life of Jesus – love, forgiveness, sacrifice, hospitality and looking after orphans and widows. After all, as Long points out, if truth is simply limited to facts, how then can we speak of God? Since God is not reduced to an object in the world, then he will not be found simply within the world of facts.[10] If we reduce God to mere facts, we have simply neglected the truth.

Long's comments are insightful as we consider the impetus behind the postliberal theological task. If truth is simply reduced to propositional correspondence, then we are allowing those purporting such a notion of truth outside our faith context to determine what we should and should not accept as truth within our faith context. Doing this allows those holding agendas contrary or at least ambivalent to questions of faith, to set the entire agenda. At the same time, the postliberal theologian should not make a blanket refusal to deny truth value to propositions altogether, but rather affirm a richer perspective of truth not merely reduced to propositional content.

Apologetics, incommensurability and religious diversity

A second substantial issue often levelled against postliberal theology concerns its apparent abandonment of apologetics for the Christian faith. But as we will see, it is not an abandonment *in toto*, but an abandonment of a certain brand of rationalistic apologetics, in favour of an ad hoc approach to demonstrate the viability of the Christian faith. Additionally, we will discuss two related problems that are linked to the issue of apologetic discourse: the problem of incommensurability of belief systems, and the challenge of inter-religious dialogue.

The absence of apologetics?

A major concern expressed with regard to postliberal theology is its absence of apologetics or lack of apparent concern for the justification of Christian beliefs. Certainly, if apologetics is about proving, defending, and bolstering one's faith on the basis of empirical, historical or rational arguments, then the agenda of a postliberal theology comes up short. We have noticed how postliberal theology is profoundly influenced by Karl Barth; its denouncing of modernist apologetics is no exception with regard to this influence. The main idea is this: Christianity will simply not be compatible with vision of reality that is foreign to a theological reality that can only be mediated by God himself. With this in mind then, can the postliberal theologian speak of justifying his or her beliefs in *any* sense?

Gary Comstock addresses this in the following:

> The task of justifying Christianity on narrativist grounds is not one of trying to show that Christian doctrines are self-evident, that Christian morality can be universal, or that its rituals of piety are archetypal. It tries to show that certain doctrines are coherent interpretations of the biblical narrative, that certain moral practices and choices 'fit' that narrative, and that specific rituals are appropriate for the community as it recalls its past and anticipates its future. For many narrativists, justification of the faith is entirely an internal, pragmatic matter.[11]

If this is the case, are the temporal, historical events recorded in the Bible completely insignificant for the postliberal theologian? No, it is not that they are insignificant, but they are not the means by which we demonstrate the value of our faith commitments or the means by which we embrace our faith. We come to Christianity within a particular community and faith tradition that has shaped our beliefs and governed our language and behaviour from within. If historical sciences govern the grammar of our faith, then we have allowed a discipline shaped by external resources that are often contrary to the embrace of faith, set the terms for the description of our faith. For postliberal theology, this is wrongheaded. Instead, the Christian faith has the same privilege of advancing its own internal narrative basis for faith as any other disciplines or sciences advocating claims of reality. The mistake is made when scientific disciplines attempt to impose their standards and methodologies of verification on a theological narrative, assuming that the same perimeters of evaluating truth or the verification of truth must be equally applied.

Alister McGrath criticizes George Lindbeck for his 'grand retreat' from history that simply reduces doctrine to an ahistorical

grammar with no specific origins. For McGrath, a theory of
doctrine must be predicated by an understanding of the origin
or 'genesis' of doctrine. Jesus is the historical source of our faith
community and our narrative. Our Christian faith and language
came about under some distinct historical conditions and must
therefore be understood in view of these developments and conditions. For McGrath, if doctrine is reduced to a cultural–linguistic
model as Lindbeck proposes, then it is not looking at the broader
historical phenomenon of doctrine as it should.[12] This is a criticism
that requires careful thought and surfaces the following question:
'Can we properly speak in a meaningful way about doctrine, if
it is not directly tied to historical events and dialogues in church
history?'

McGrath submits that doctrine does not simply provide the
grammar or discourse of the faith community, but it actually
defines the community. It creates the identity of the community;
it helps prescribe the conditions of entry into the community,
and justifies the community before rival communities. McGrath
concedes, however, that the early Christian communities did not
have an elaborate doctrinal statement. However, they still displayed
certain doctrinal distinctions within their communities that were,
in a sense, imposed on them by the outside world because of the
Christian community's particular views about Jesus. They also
needed to define themselves with respect to and as distinct from
Judaism. For McGrath, this particular history is essential for the
analysis of doctrine and how it took shape. Unlike that which he
sees in Lindbeck's approach, the historical phenomena surrounding
doctrine must be carefully considered and nuanced.[13] Historical
factors in the formation of what we call doctrine are simply much
more important for McGrath than he perceives is the case for
Lindbeck.

How important are the details of historical truth for our
Christian faith and what purpose do such details serve? For some
Christians, every precise detail of the biblical stories is critical for
the truth of our faith. For others, the stories are reduced to moral
examples and the technicalities of historical events are more or
less negligible. Postliberal theologians such as Frei and Lindbeck
certainly understood these divergent tendencies in fundamentalist
conservatism and liberalism in their respective projects, but they
sought a middle ground. Detailed historical analysis is obviously

not the major priority of their work, but this does not mean that some clear sense of historical rootedness is completely lost. However, if the Bible is reduced to a history book, it will never have a radical effect on our lives in Christian community today, as it should. Neither can the Bible narrative be reduced to a mere collection of moral lessons.[14] The history is important, but so is the truth about how we fit into that history in our current faith communities.

In this manner, Richard Crane points out that postliberals embrace 'historicist interpretations of human rationality' when they argue that all reasoning occurs within certain contexts, traditions and assumptions of particular cultures or backgrounds. It is very complex how we obtain good reasons for belief in something; there are many factors, none of which is neutral. The biblical narrative truthfully provides the narrative of the real world in which we live, but this does not mean that it is built on some common, universally understood foundations.[15] As we said before, this does not mean that the issue of truth is avoided, but it is simply addressed from a different angle of understanding. Truth is always a term that is used as a pointer to reality, but the definition of reality must not be determined by forces outside the faith context.

With a postliberal understanding of truth, we return to our question: Is there is any need for Christian apologetics or defense of the Christian faith? Well, if doing apologetics implies that we must provide an empirical, historical or rational justification for faith prior to accepting that faith, then apologetics is misguided. Likewise, if apologetic justification is seen as a necessary condition in order to claim the value of Christian faith in 'respectable fashion' before one's culture or society, then this is also misguided. Such assumptions are simply allowing secular and modernistic intellectual agendas to set the ground rules for what is or is not valuable for Christians to believe. Furthermore, if Christians invariably attempt to meet the demands of justification imposed on them from non-Christian paradigms, the demands will never be fully met or satisfied. Mere empirical and rational agendas cannot disclose all reality or understanding; they are both intellectually and morally insufficient to do so. If intellectual methods are grounded in secular ideals (which are inherently not religious or intended to be) then using such methods will never arrive at the desired goal of religious faith. At this primary level then, systematic apologetics is neither needed nor desired for a postliberal theology.

A call for ad hoc apologetics

Hans Frei acknowledges that Christian theologians and philosophers of religion have long desired to show the credibility of
their theology to contemporary thinkers from the beginning of
the 1700s. Apologetic procedures throughout this history have
consisted of basic common patterns. These would include such
matters as demonstrating the truthfulness of the Gospel narrative,
plus various proofs, both rational and physical, for the existence
of God. These factors have been considered indispensable because
they are considered essential for the 'essence' of Christianity. But
as Frei points out, others take a less evidential approach to apologetics. This group claims that Christianity is only understood by
those who willingly submit themselves to the distinctive practices
of the faith and are willing to live as Christians. The moral
influence that accompanies such practices, then, would provide the
persuasive power of the Christian faith. In this regard, the apologetic is found in the commitment and practice itself. Frei himself
is convinced that the attempt to systematically demonstrate the
meaningfulness of Christianity through such apologetic endeavours
is misplaced and even 'self-defeating' unless it is done in an ad hoc
fashion, as we mentioned previously. In saying this, however, Frei
is not trying to imply that Christianity is illogical. He simply does
not personally wish to speculate on the evidential arguments, for
example with regard to the Resurrection of Jesus, even though he
would affirm that it is an essential claim for Christianity. But in
affirming it as an essential claim, the Resurrection is nonetheless
unlike other types of factual statement in that it 'shapes a new
life'.[16]

It is important to stress again that Frei, along with other
postliberal theologians, is not denying claims of truth for the essentials of Christianity. Rather, he is calling for a separation between
what is deemed 'meaningful' in Christian dogma and that which
is represented in apologetic argumentation.[17] However, his views
on apologetic endeavors are certainly coloured by the fact that he
does not believe that there is a 'single road to Christianity'. If one's
convictions are as such, then apologetic efforts are clearly inconsequential. Just the same, Frei is still not denying truth statements
of the Christian faith, such as the resurrection of Christ; in fact, he

seems to affirm their necessity. But, for Frei's purposes, he does not see the need to bother with proving them in some demonstrable fashion, neither does he believe such verification-centred apologetic efforts will inherently affect the narrative of Jesus that shapes new life.

Postliberal theologian William Placher affirms, along with Hans Frei, that there is indeed room for ad hoc apologetics with a postliberal theology.[18] Contra to the presuppositions of modernity, this apologetic approach does not begin by looking for universal notions or conditions to set the agenda for agreement in argumentation. There simply cannot be a common notion of understanding of a pre-described world between the Christian and non-Christian. If there were, it would imply the ability of the Christian to step outside of her already given world in community to some sort of neutral zone of communication. As we have already noted, this is impossible with a postliberal theology. This does not mean there is no common ground for conversation. As humans, we are communicative beings and our communication practices can form points of contact that allow degrees of common ground. This assumes, of course, that there is a linguistic world of sorts that is to some degree mutually accessible. At the same time, as we have pointed out, 'truth' is not reducible to such common understanding in discourse.[19] All discourse to some degree or another remains an incomplete representation of the world we encounter through our experience and practice. Words, facts, and propositions may be pointers to reality, but always in need of appropriation within community practice to be more fully understood. The practice of truth is no small part of understanding and proclaiming truth itself.

Apologetics that appeals to some form of presupposed universal reason is contrary to faith for the postliberal. Instead, Christians must demonstrate the coherence between Christian beliefs and practices, and encourage non-Christians to become absorbed and rooted into the practices, grammar and faith of Christian community. When this happens, it will ultimately have an apologetic appeal. This 'appeal' does not validate or prove Christianity to the observer though by making it simply 'relevant' to the non-Christian world;[20] but the faith of the Christian community may nonetheless be extremely persuasive in this regard.

Can postliberal theology in any meaningful way adjudicate between competing claims of truth or competing claims of religious faith? The postliberal may point out that Christians come to faith within the context of Christian community and then practise their faith within the community as followers of Jesus. So practice reinforces and creates the conditions for belief, just as the ongoing beliefs of the community continue to reinforce the patterns of practice within that community. However, some persistent questions remain. What about those living apart from such communities of faith who do not seem have any sense of community? Or what about those who have been abandoned or hurt deeply by a local community? How does a postliberal theology help those genuinely seeking religious truth among multiple welcoming communities, some of which may not be Christian oriented at all?

Lindbeck addresses this issue with respect to his perspective of ad hoc apologetics when it comes to diverse religious claims. Christians are versed in their particular language and community with their own grammatical rules of doctrine that shape their identity and expression. The Christian religion is like a language in this regard, so it cannot be completely translatable any more than other languages such as French or Swahili. Words, phrases and particular idioms can be conveyed at different levels of accuracy, but simply listening to translations will not give the full impact and level of understanding as if you are a 'native' speaker who is completely immersed in the culture and language of the given tongue. Different cultures, as with different religions, approach reality with a different set of lenses that organize and categorize the reality experienced and observed. So the outcomes on what reality 'truly is' will be different. Due to the radical particularity of religious beliefs, various levels of incommensurability will always remain. Nevertheless, Lindbeck still argues: 'Resistance to translation does not wholly exclude apologetics, but this must be of an ad hoc and nonfoundational variety rather than standing at the center of theology. The grammar of religion, like that of language, cannot be explicated or learned by analysis of experience, but only by practice.'[21] The answers that are given to apologetically related questions would depend on the character of the one asking the question and the character of the questions themselves. In many cases, people become followers of Christ after their other 'options' have fallen apart. To some antagonists of Christianity, one set of answers will be given; to others a different set of answers may be appropriate. There is not a 'one-size-fits-all' approach to apologetics. The variety of ways in which the Holy Spirit works is as different as there is variety of people and backgrounds. Regardless, for the postliberal theologian, it is impossible to step completely outside Christian faith in order to 'objectively' compare a different faith commitment or religion.[22] This impossibility, however, must not be seen as a concession to weakness, as if objectivity were the aspired goal for arbitration between different or seemingly competing views. Stepping outside one's faith context is not only impossible, it is not even desirable. For it is our faith context that gives us access to the world and its differences, so it must be embraced as such.

Problem of incommensurability and apologetic discourse

Granted, you must be embedded, immersed and living within the context of the language to have the best possible understanding of that language. But as Lindbeck noted, this does not preclude any contact whatsoever. But the ad hoc apologetic approach works from intratextual description with an insider's perspective, rather than assuming a general philosophical scheme to which differing parties must subscribe.[23]

The question remains as to whether such a descriptive approach is in any meaningful way truly *apologetic* in helping with the problem of incommensurability. Can those attempting to adjudicate between religious claims offer judgements on particular religious perspectives? Lindbeck, again drawing on Wittgenstein and Kuhn, argues that we cannot appeal to some general theory of reason in order to substantiate religious claims because the norms of what is deemed reasonable are too complex and diverse to be specified in this way. But this does not mean that religious beliefs are simply reduced to relativism or irrationalism. Reason still places constraints on religious perspectives, for Lindbeck, even if such constraints cannot be precisely identified. But to have some level of understanding of these constraints one must not look to some universal or independent criteria, but from skill of performance of the religion. The confirmation or denial of a religion comes from the repetition of success (or failure) in making the beliefs practical and coherent. This process continues on through history unless the particular community of religious faith disappears.[24] In our estimation, Lindbeck is a bit confusing at this juncture. In his denial of universal or independent criteria for evaluating religion outside of religion, he seems to be suggesting that the evaluation of success or failure of a given religion, or at least the estimation of its disappearance, would imply some notion of external universally centred standards of assessment.

Nonetheless, within this framework, Lindbeck affirms a postliberal ad hoc approach to apologetic discourse in terms of what it denies. It would exclude an approach, so he claims:

> that is systematically prior and controlling in the fashion of post-Cartesian natural theology and of later liberalism. As Aquinas himself notes, reasoning in support of the faith is not meritorious before faith, but only afterward, or, in the conceptuality employed in this book, the logic of coming to believe, because it is like that of learning a language, has little room for argument, but once one has learned to speak the language of faith, argument becomes possible.[25]

Lindbeck claims that this approach is nothing new, as this is the way the Christian faith has been passed on throughout Church history. It is faith first, followed by understanding. Whether from good motive or bad, pagan converts to Christianity were attracted to the life and vitality of the Christian community. But in the process they learned the practices, beliefs and language of the community. They learned the stories of the Old Testament and how the promises of Israel come to fruition in Christ.[26] They lived within the narrative of scripture that became lived out and practised in the Christian community.

Interreligious dialogue

Neither a cognitive–propositional nor an experiential–expressivist approach to theology may sustain the challenge of interreligious dialogue. This is exactly the criticism that assaults postliberal theology because of its apparent isolationist mentality. The cognitive–propositional theologian will insist on a mentality of universal reason: once a doctrine is proclaimed true, then it will always be true. The experiential–expressivist will simply contend that doctrines do not make truth claims anyway; they are instead expressions of existential feelings. Lindbeck's cultural–linguistic approach attempts to navigate between these extremes by saying that every religious tradition has its own grammar for its particular community of faith. There is indeed an inherent incommensurability. There are no general overarching rules that govern all religious communities or determine what is or is not regulative for a specific community. When considering the subject of inter-religious dialogue, for Lindbeck in particular, it is essential to remember what seems to be an implicit underlying concern in his project: ecumenical dialogue. For Lindbeck, the ecumenist will help those of varying faith communities better understand their own rules or grammar of faith.[27]

We referred earlier to Janine Fletcher's work on Lindbeck on the possibility of interreligious dialogue. Fletcher suggests that we can agree with Lindbeck on the radical breakdown in communication that occurs in religious dialogue, due to different perspectives and backgrounds of religious traditions. However, she suggests that these moments of 'disorientation' and lack of understanding with the unknown are 'theologically fruitful' for stimulating us to remember the wonder and 'incomprehensible mystery of God', along with our own human limitations when it comes to adequately describing God. In fact, Fletcher suggests that the basic point we can learn in interreligious dialogue is being able to confess to the other that we do not understand them. In this, we promote dialogue and posture ourselves to better understand the other and appreciate her differences.[28] Fletcher is certainly right in saying that God is beyond our control and limited imagination within our respective traditions. How we posture ourselves in our discussions is extremely important for initiating and maintaining both intentional and ad hoc opportunities for interreligious dialogue and understanding.

It may be helpful at this juncture to reconsider several insights from one of the previously highlighted philosophical precursors to postliberal theological thought, the ethicist/philosopher, Alasdair MacIntyre. As we recall, MacIntyre argues that there is no way to engage in reasoned or rational justification or rejection of certain beliefs apart from the standpoint of a particular tradition.

However, it is still the case that 'competing traditions' share some standards and hold to some agreement in logic. If this were not so, they could not actually disagree in the ways that they do. But the agreements they do share are not enough to resolve disagreements. Various traditions have their own particular standards for what is considered reasonable based on background beliefs. There are two major challenges that stem from these considerations, according to MacIntyre: the relativist challenge and the perspectivist challenge. The relativist claims that no particular tradition can deny or exclude another tradition in the name of exclusivity. The perspectivist solution is to withdraw the notions of 'truth' and 'falsity' as they have typically been used. Rather than viewing traditions as inherently incompatible systems, the perspectivist wants us to notice complementary ways of viewing the world. MacIntyre's point on both the relativist and perspectivist challenge is that neither arose to provide a critical response to truth claims, but both challenges are 'fundamentally misconceived and misdirected'. This is due of their reliance on a particular type of Enlightenment-generated view of truth that is guaranteed by supposed universally acclaimed rational methods of verification. For the relativist or perspectivist, since a rational methodology cannot be maintained, relativism or perspectivism is the only option. In this way, MacIntyre submits, relativism and perspectivism are simply a 'negative counterpart' or 'inverted mirror image' of the same Enlightenment thinking. Proponents of such views have prided themselves on being contra-Enlightenment, yet in many ways are heirs of the same presuppositions. But ultimately, what neither view is able to do is distinguish the particular kind of rationality that is essential to traditions themselves.[29]

As notable as his efforts are in identifying this latent 'haunting' of Enlightenment rationalism even on such systems that claim to oppose it, we are left wondering if it is essential to suggest that tradition based rationality must necessarily be designated 'rationality' at all. Does not MacIntyre himself betray a tie to Enlightenment assumptions by his attempt to reframe the notion of rationality itself? Can it not be the case that we come to understanding of reality by other means than that which is esteemed or labelled as 'rational'? Furthermore, when we come to the heart of MacIntyre's efforts in this regard, it seems problematic to apply typical understandings of rationality. MacIntyre's tradition-laden rationality fails the Cartesian test for rationality, as there are not indubitable and self-evident truths, while it fails the Hegelian test in that there is not some ultimate rationality that is shared among all. If one has been taught that anything worth speaking intelligibly must pass either of these 'ultimate' tests, then tradition will be readily accused of simply being arbitrary.[30]

But a tradition is always a form of enquiry, for MacIntyre. Just the same, it will still advocate certain intellectual virtues and claim that certain methods are better than others. Also, there will come a time when some will perceive things differently than others within a particular tradition and they will henceforth need to frame their own method of enquiry. What will always prevail with multiple contexts of proposed 'truth' will be 'the appeal to authority of established belief'. As MacIntrye submits: 'The incoherence within established belief will always provide a reason for enquiring further, but not in itself a conclusive reason for rejecting established belief, until something more adequate because less incoherent has been discovered.'[31] So, the rationality of traditions is marked by both 'contingency and positivity'. Traditions are still rational because they are marked by a dialectical historical process that provides an ongoing process of justification. Granted, it is not an absolutist type of epistemological justification, but a justification that is continually questioned, reformulated and reconceived and further justified.[32] Whether or not one agrees with MacIntyre's conclusions, his observations regarding the impossibility of some neutral, tradition-independent religious dialogue and the bankruptcy of both perspectivism and relativism are quite helpful in relation to understanding postliberal theological thought as it relates to inter-religious dialogue.

Although he is not particularly reasoning from a postliberal perspective, Amos Yong argues that Christians, with the presence of the Holy Spirit, should take a humble posture in interfaith dialogue, displaying an openness and honesty about their sinfulness and finitude, while affirming the image of God in each person. This stems from a basic pneumatological vision and conviction that Christians should have about the Spirit of God being 'universally present and active'. Thus, he claims that we should not exclude a priori any voices or perspectives from engaging in conversation.[33] Of course, engagement in conversation and dialogue does not imply agreement, but it certainly should imply a certain degree of cordiality. If indeed the image of God is characteristic of all human beings, than there is something significant about each human being that is worth consideration pertaining to one's affections, concerns and worldviews. Being willing to learn from those of different faith traditions, based on this understanding, while maintaining commitment to one's particular faith community, is the noble challenge.

Gerald R. McDermott submits that the scandal of particularity, that is the particular revelation and expression (and postliberals would certainly add 'practice') of the Christian faith in history, will be the biggest challenge for the church in this century. Why Jesus? Why not Muhammad or the Buddha? And if we provide simply stated astute apologetic rebuffs to other religions in today's radically diverse societies, McDermott claims that 'the church's message will be a scandal not of particularity but of arrogant obscurantism.'[34] It is tragic if those outside our faith context are simply relegated to the enemy camp without respectful dialogue and compassion.

Remaining committed to our faith context does not imply that ad hoc, authentic dialogue may not take place with other faith perspectives. As we mentioned in the introduction, Philip Kenneson suggests that the basic grammar of the community includes a commitment to reformation always seeking reformation (*ecclesia semper reformanda*). If this is so, then it is reasonable to suggest that even within postliberal theological perspective, the Church community can dialogue and learn from those outside its particular faith context. It is not that interpretive communities are isolationist, but they are embedded within a community that provides them with an angle to access the world, not a means by which to close it off from access altogether. In this regard, it provides a way to organize the phenomena of the world in such a way to be an effective instrument of change. In a postliberal context, this will unashamedly be within a robustly Christian framework in a particular faith tradition. With interreligious dialogue, as with apologetic efforts in general for the postliberal, efforts are not made to seek some sort of presumed neutrality to reach a common underlying truth. Whatever is learned from another faith tradition will be coloured and marked from the lens of our own faith community and will remain distinctly Christian. Just the same, we are learning something of the other faith as we are compelled to seek understanding of our community while in the midst of many others.[35]

It may seem surprising that the premier theological forerunner of postliberal theology – Karl Barth – himself suggested that some revelations occur outside the context of the Bible and the Church:

> We recognize that the fact that Jesus Christ is the one Word of God does not mean that in the Bible, the Church and the world there are not other words which are quite notable in their way, other lights which are quite clear and other revelations which are quite real. ... Nor does it follow from our statement that that every word spoken outside the circle of the Bible and the Church is a word of false prophecy and therefore valueless, empty and corrupt, that all the lights which rise and shine in this outer sphere are misleading and all the revelations are necessarily untrue. Our statement is simply to the effect that Jesus Christ is the one and only Word of God, that He alone is the light of God and the revelation of God.[36]

Indeed, for Barth, the ultimate truth of God only comes directly from God through Jesus Christ. But Jesus is Lord of all and 'He exercises authority in this outer as well as inner sphere and is free to attest Himself or to cause Himself to be attested in it.'[37] One thing is certain for Barth, however the truth of God is communicated, if it is indeed the truth of God; it is communicated via Jesus Christ.

Within the context of a faith that refuses to yield to epistemological pressures of systems outside the faith, Barth still opens up a space in which the world is God's playground, understanding he can communicate to whom and through whomever He chooses. Barth not only saw the possibility of truths revealed from outside the faith context but he also rebaptized some for his own purposes. Citing the research of George Hunsinger, Gerald McDermott points out that Barth recast the Hellenistic concept of being and applied it to the vitality of the living God. He also reframed the notion of existential nothingness to correspond with the biblical idea of chaos, that which is contrary to the ultimate goodness of Creation.[38] We must not conclude from these reflections that Barth is condoning interreligious apologetic dialogue by bolstering arguments to demonstrate the correspondence between Christianity and other religions. At the same time, we are suggesting that a postliberal appropriation of Barth in this respect is neither adverse nor contrary to interreligious dialogue. In fact, it may actually demonstrate the strength of an intratextual commitment for effective theological communication.

Now some may still object that conversational or dialogical ad hoc apologetic connections do not appeal to the ethical call of a particular religious faith, in this case the Christian faith. Janine Fletcher's challenge to promote dialogue through genuine, humble posturing is noble and certainly must be practised. There are certainly areas in which religions other than our own may reveal aspects of the mystery of God that we have neglected or overlooked. But is this the entire point of theology? Certainly this may be the case, but we must not concede on the distinctiveness of our beliefs either.

Postliberal theologian William Placher suggests that in serious interaction with non-Christian voices, that a preservation of our distinct Christian voice must remain intact amidst the politically correct movement seeking some 'common core to all religions'.[39] As noted earlier, Lindbeck claimed that our evaluation of the intelligibility for the acceptance of a religion stems from its success in practice throughout history. But we must be careful not to generalize from this assertion that all postliberal theologians would simply say that *how* our religion is evaluated leads to a determination of its truth. It seems that Stanley Hauerwas comes close to this when he claims that the 'truthfulness of Jesus creates and is known by the kind of community his story should form'.[40] If Hauerwas were to specifically explain what he means by 'truth' in this context it would be more instructive. At first glance, Placher disagrees with Hauerwas. If it is simply the virtues of people that make the narratives true by way of some sort of empirical validation, then we could easily fall prey to an extreme relativism. If the community practices do not at some point reflect proper virtues of Christianity, would this render the beliefs themselves false? Placher would rather avoid such arguments along these lines altogether.[41] We must be cautious with the pragmatic claims that are strongly emphasized in Hauerwas and to some extent by Lindbeck. If the proof is only in the pudding, so to speak, and the pudding is distasteful, then is the recipe mistaken? Most certainly not so if the recipe for the Christian faith is rather found in the person of Jesus – the incarnate God – and his intentions for the community of the Church. The community of faith will always be an imperfect translation, yet nonetheless embodied application, of Jesus' inauguration of the Kingdom of God.

Relating to culture and the public sphere

Another concern that essentially stems from the criticisms of truth, apologetics and interreligious dialogue, is that of the ability of postliberal theology to relate to the broader culture and public sphere. What is it that prevents a postliberal approach from insularism? Is there any room for public debate at all? I believe these questions may be addressed in the form of two basic answers, which in part have already been reflected in the previous sections on truth and apologetics. We will nonetheless address this particular question more specifically.

First of all, these questions presuppose the inherent value in the need to relate to culture and the public sphere. Perhaps the question that must first be addressed is this: is it absolutely necessary *to* relate to culture? If this is simply assumed to be the case, without further reflection, then would we not be simply yielding to the same external influence of accepted, generalized public systems that postliberal theology is so desperately attempting to avoid by being '*post*'-liberal? Christians are indeed called to be a witness to the world, to do good works, and to be a light shining in the darkness, all of which may at times require certain alliances with those who are non-Christians or those embracing other faith traditions. However, this does not preclude active criticism of culture or even a separation from culture for the sake of the Christian gospel. As William Placher adds: 'Perhaps, in service of such a witness, even a modest dose of sectarianism is not such a terrible thing. Perhaps those whose particular calling is the strange task of theology can even be forgiven for being postliberal theologians.'[42] Of course, even Placher's statement betrays a tongue-in-cheek acknowledgement of the felt need to justify *why* a postliberal theology must remain to some degree sectarian. At the same time, Placher is suggesting that postliberal sectarian practice in itself may present a powerful witness to contemporary culture.

Placher points out that this is also the approach of Stanley Hauerwas. The Christian community, by the sake of it being a Christian community, provides a persuasive impact on society. By remaining committed to one's Christian tradition and acting responsibly within that tradition, the public sphere will be positively influenced.[43] We believe both Placher and Hauerwas are both correct on this. A devoted Christian community will be involved in doing good works that will affect the broader society. Additionally, the activity of 'being' community itself will provide a powerful witness as to the meaningfulness of that community itself.

Such radical sectarian influence was radically brought to light by the tragic shooting incident among the Amish in Lancaster County, Pennsylvania, at the Nickel Mines School in October, 2006. A local milk truck driver, Charles Roberts IV, entered the one-room schoolhouse and took young girls between 6 and 13 years old as hostages. He shot ten of the girls, five of whom were dead before he shot himself in an act of suicide. It was a senseless, violent act of evil. The reaction from the Amish community was absolutely unbelievable. Their response of forgiveness astonished the media, the nation and the world. In fact, within hours of the shooting, the Amish were expressing words of forgiveness to the widow of the gunman, as well as to his parents. Even more outstanding and shocking was that the Amish gave a proportion of the funds they received to help with the suffering families in their community to the widow and children of the assailant, Charles Roberts. But it does not stop there; the story of forgiveness continues. More than half of the people in attendance at Roberts' funeral were Amish families – there to show grace to Roberts' family.[44]

Anger was not to be found among these Amish families towards the killer, but only deep sorrow and pain. One may argue that grief and anger often go together or that the expressed forgiveness from the Amish came much too suddenly. But this criticism fails to see that 'forgiveness is woven into the fabric of the Amish culture' and it was fully decided 'by their history and religious beliefs'. This does not mean it was necessarily easy for them, simply because forgiveness was expressed quickly. One father who lost his daughter in the shooting admitted that he must start over with forgiveness every day. This absolutely amazing reaction and authentic practice of grace and forgiveness spurred some 2400 stories in the media that focused more on the courage to forgive in the wake of horror, than they did about the violent act itself.[45] Grace and forgiveness from within a vibrant community of faith is more powerful than shockingly evil acts of violence from without.

This is a remarkable example of how a commitment to one's faith, fully embedded in narrative and tradition of that faith, even within (what is often seen as) an extreme sectarian context, may still have a radically profound impact on society. The Amish are certainly no friends to modern culture and society. In fact, many would say that they do not relate at all to the public sphere. They stay to themselves in most aspects of life, simply acting consistently and faithfully within their faith context in their community. With no regard for society's values or acts of self-aggrandizement, a faithfully devout community can still have a powerful effect on that society. There are, of course, many bad examples of 'extreme' sectarian religious perspectives that have caused abuse and corruption and, in turn, have had an extremely negative impact on culture and society. But cases of misappropriated authority and dissent from the truly Christian faith community narrative surely do not negate the value of rightly appropriated commitments and Christian virtues in the faith community of the Church and their redemptive effects on society at large.

Second, a postliberal approach to theology does not preclude the ability to relate to cultural and public issues that are to some extent outside the particular grammar and function of one's faith. The Christian faith is not completely relegated to a private world, isolated from broader concerns of the world, but it may be seen as functioning in a different manner for different aspects of life. Just as Wittgenstein's language games functioned in different spheres of life's activities, so our Christian practices and language games within our Christian narrative operate differently at times than do aspects of life within the context of the broader culture. It is not that the two can never meet, but when they do meet, the grammar may not readily be commensurate for both contexts. The language of faith will not necessarily enter the language of the kitchen, garage or business deal. This does not mean that faith is contradictory or inappropriate to maintain. Neither does this imply that one's faith will be exempt from influence throughout all areas of life's concern. As Kathryn Tanner submits:

> By infiltrating Christians' activities with other Christians, by being brought inside, those other roles and commitments are

reworked in the course of such activities. Christians, moreover, remain in social interactions with non-Christians; they engage with any non-Christian sites of social interaction that might exist. Their Christian commitments remain relevant to these spheres, too, and therefore operate to transform the character of social relations in them. In such fashions, prophetic objections to the wider society are maintained, not by isolation, but by the indefinitely extended effort to alter, where necessary, whatever one comes across through sustained engagement with it, in and out of church.[46]

In this manner, the church is the embodied and continuing narrative of Jesus – a Jesus not simply of word, but of flesh and blood in the world. As Jesus did, so we must do; with concrete, practical expressions of our faith even to the 'least of these'. Stanley Hauerwas emphasized that our Christian identity in community is an activity of embodying Christ, not simply a precondition for that identity.[47] The church as the body of Christ is not simply an indicative declaration, but it is at least partially the means by which this identification is established. It is a living body, which means it moves and acts according to it being 'a body'.

Michael Higton's profound work on Hans Frei, *Christ, Providence and History*, argues that Frei was essentially a 'public' theologian, even if theology must speak from a particular embedded understanding not shared by the public. Theology may be beyond 'public proof,' but it will always make 'public sense' in the context of public discourse. After all, theology takes place in history and history is God working providentially through Jesus Christ. But to take theology in this way, means that it must not be so caught up in complex methodological concerns. We will always do better speaking about history than the theoretical explanations of how to speak about it. Sophisticated methodological concerns are the curse of modernity for Frei and they have provided little benefits. The mere fact that Christians have been able to see God's work in the Gospels through Jesus and also see God working through current events in our historical context today in light of theological commentary, clearly shows that the Spirit of God works more broadly than we often imagine. These aspects of God working have been held together by Christians who have lived their lives 'fallibly but well in the public world'. Frei devoted his theological and historical work to continue this task.[48]

Postliberals may be accused of being isolationist or sectarian, as a movement advocating a retreat from external worldly influences that seek to corrupt the Christian faith or worldview, forcing an unholy compromise their views. As Higton's research points out with Frei, this is an unfortunate exaggeration and misrepresentation. Does the 'external world' really impose its perspectives on the Christian community in such a manner as this? Instead, as Philip Kenneson argues, competing views of the 'external' world often show up even within the Church itself. Perhaps a good share of the time, such 'external' influences are not as much secular, as much as they are a part of the dynamic narrative character of the Church community and God's interactive relationship with His people as they engage with God's world.[49] The Christian Church has always been host itself to myriad perspectives on the views of the world in which we live and move, from science to ecology or politics. This diversity within the Church will remain just as diversity outside the Church.

The Church need not be isolationist to remain particular in its expression and practice of faith. But any hint of particularity is often contrary to the political correctness of our day. If the 'world's' narratives are to be subsumed within the narrative of the Church as postliberals would have it, then this flies in the face of the notion that many stories are always better and where each story must be esteemed equally by all. If a particular narrative were in some way promoted over another, the spirit of political correctness would have us believe that this will lead to radical fundamentalism, closed-mindedness and violence towards the other.[50] The powerful story of the Amish families' treatment of Charles Roberts is a powerful demonstration that this does not follow. The Church can embrace diversity and difference from within and without. It may not look like the type of diversity and soft 'tolerance' that a politically correct society may wish to tout, pretending as if there were some agenda-less neutrality. However, it is more intellectually honest. It recognizes that we all approach our beliefs and understandings from a background or community that shapes us. Neutrality is impossible. Rather than viewing our background as something to shun, postliberals see it as something to embrace. It is through the background of the Christian community and its particularity where the practice of faith may flourish to move beyond isolationism.

The diversity among Christian communities is nonetheless quite varied in its church practice and expression of spirituality, despite some very common ancient creedal commitments and common practices. So we are not suggesting that there is some overarching grand ecumenism that has maintained the spirit of unity across various Christian faith expressions. This is far from the truth. But the process of reconciliation among various faith expressions continues to be a vital, vibrant struggle throughout the Christian Church among Roman Catholics, Lutherans, Pentecostals and many others from inside and outside various ecumenical organizations. This ongoing struggle itself demonstrates how postliberals may continue to counter accusations of isolationism. They can influence the public sphere, if not directly and explicitly, at least implicitly, through the seeking of unity in a religiously fragmented and often religiously apathetic culture.

CHAPTER 5

Prospects and proposals for postliberal theology today

In the midst of our descriptions and basic analyses, we have not shunned from highlighting positive features or criticisms of postliberal theology or its representatives. However, this chapter will focus more specifically on the most promising aspects and contributions of the movement, engaging some of its derivative theological applications, while extending its insights for ongoing service to the church today and into the future. At the same time, we will express some cautions pertaining to tendencies of postliberal theology that must be avoided. James Fodor has suggested that the contributions of postliberal theology 'are best understood in terms of retrieval, repair, and renewal'. It is not a movement or mood promising brand new insights, but rather it is advocating reform, correction and ecumenical regeneration. With this in mind, we offer the following observations for reinforcing and augmenting various key aspects of postliberal theology. This is done with the intention of stimulating discussion for an ongoing critical dialogue about and critical appropriation of this rich movement in years to come.

Chastened rationality and recovery of humanity: head and heart

Postliberal theology effectively responds to the postmodern refusal to let empiricism and rationalism set the agenda and dictate the terms for our Christian faith. It tacitly asks: why must we make our faith subservient to an externally imposed view of reality and allow it to dictate *our* understanding of reality and the shape of our theology?

Essentially, modernism has robbed human beings of their full humanity by simply reducing them to thinking animals. Postliberal theology attempts a recovery of our humanity by recognizing that we are narratival, affective beings. We are people whose hearts are often governed by our affections and loves and those affections and loves are formed within and from our practices in the institutions of our Church communities. We are not mere brains trapped in our bodies, as Cartesian reductionist anthropology would espouse. Instead, we are complex embodied beings that feel, think, imagine, dream, have emotions and have the need to practise these qualities in the context of community. This is clearly the picture of humanity we find in scripture. James K. A. Smith articulates this brilliantly when he writes the following:

> An incarnational anthropology begins with the affirmation that human persons are material; that we don't just inhabit flesh and blood, but we *are* flesh and blood. Being embodied is an essential feature of being a human creature. As such we are not defined by thinking; rather, we are primarily affective: the center of the person is not the mind, but the heart. (That's not to say we are irrational, but only that rationality [mind] is relative to what Augustine calls 'the right order of love'—the direction of our heart.)[1]

Although Smith is not directly referring to postliberal tendencies, but it is fair to say that we readily notice his latent (even if reworked) sympathies with the movement.

If we truly understand this affective aspect our humanity, then we will see the connection between our embodied everyday practices in the Church community and their formative value on our character as the people of God. As God in-fleshed into the narrative of our world, so we live out the embodied Christ in that ongoing narrative of the Church, as diverse as it is. We are complex, emotional, thinking creatures that are embedded in a community. But this community is not a monolithic structure of oneness, but of diversity. The Church is characterized by its diversity with unity. This is the nature of the living, ongoing embodiment of Christ in its rich manifestation in the Church.

Although not referring specifically to postliberal theology, William Cavanaugh has argued that the religion/reason or religious/secular opposition is an invention of modernism. Religion is not, as it is often mistaken to be, beyond history, culture and human rationality. As he puts it succinctly, 'Religion as passionate and non-rational is not a fact but a construction of the modern West.'[2] For Cavanaugh it is precisely this misunderstanding that has blamed religion as irrational and fanatical, hence responsible for the violence that has erupted throughout history in the name of religion.[3] This unwarranted division between head and heart that Cavanaugh points out is responsible for a host of theological and philosophical errors in our thinking and ecclesiological practice. An appropriation of postliberal theology provides a space for a robust contemporary theology that can embrace strong habits of intellectual engagement while at the same time stimulate active, reflective and emotionally engaged behaviour within particular communities of the Church. Let us be storying people who embrace the biblical narrative in community, acknowledging that we are a people who used logic and reasoning within our stories.

Of course, our faith cannot be reduced to stories, experiences, and affections any more that it can be reduced to logic and rational propositions. A postliberal theology that abandons critical reflection altogether in the name of story and narrative is also denying the fact that careful critical thinking has been a part of the language of the community that has afforded us the opportunity to reflect on the origins of the storying community itself. Smith and Cavanaugh both remind us that the division between our head and heart is an unhealthy fabrication of modernism. Smith specifically challenges us to see that our rational propositions are all caught up in our affections. It is not an either/or matter, but always both/and. This is not a bad thing; it is simply the way we are created as rationally emotive human beings. Unfortunately, we tend to be people who often misappropriate the extremes on either end.

Many conservative biblicists, so it seems, have taken a 'vitamin' approach to scripture. The Bible has become a collection of little snippet vitamins or propositional energy bars by which to feed the soul with daily nourishment. Your spirituality for the day is determined by whether or not you have moved your eyes over a page or passage of the Bible. Once this happens, you are ready to begin your day. Other liberal approaches may not care as much about reading the Bible, as much as they care about applying the existential lessons encased in the heart of the biblical stories. Both approaches tend to separate the head from the heart, as we discussed earlier, and they neglect a full-orbed view of biblical anthropology, hence neglecting the reality and truth of the biblical narrative. The biblical narrative has value in and of itself; it may not be flattened out as a mere device to produce a faith lesson for our existence (liberal) or faith application and defence from its history (conservative). It is story, and must be embraced as our story as we are the people of God through whom His ongoing story is told.

Affections and liturgical practices

A renewed application of postliberal theology today will recognize that we are affective people, immersed in stories and storying practices. Since we are both rational and affective beings at the same time (with all that entails: logic, emotions, imaginations, sense of beauty) it means that our Christian faith must not merely take shape in a propositional or experiential context. Rather, it must include propositions *and* other qualities of speech acts in the context of the narrative of the Bible and its ongoing practice in the community of faith. James K. A. Smith again insightfully argues that our liturgical practices 'whether "sacred" or "secular"–shape and constitute our identities by forming our most fundamental desires and our most basic attunement to the world.'[4] These insights are extremely pertinent for the ongoing applicability and development of postliberal theology. Postliberal theological expressions move this direction by bringing back the focus of story and narrative as our 'reality' instead of dismissing them as inconsequential to our humanity. Rather than allowing external, modernity-driven systems of knowledge and pedagogy that stem from a God-absent worldview set the terms, postliberal theology embraces the narrative structure of our humanness as it is. Again, a postliberal theology does not and, indeed, should not ignore that we are also rationally minded creatures. But it refuses to tolerate a vision of humanity that reduces humanity or the communication patterns of humans to mere rationality. It will not allow an external structure determined by culture or current intellectual trends to be imposed on it indiscriminately.

As 'storying' people we participate in 'storying' practices that characterize our humanity – we have memories, hopes, celebrations, feelings, with desires for community, family and love. These practices, which Smith calls 'liturgies', shape our desires or loves by directing our affections through our bodies. Liturgies make us the kind of people that we are because we are fundamentally creatures of desire, love and hope.[5] It is through practice and liturgy that we are formed into the Christians we are intended to be. Praise is prior to theological analysis, as praying comes prior to thinking. We are primarily 'loving, desiring, affective, liturgical animals who, for the most part, don't inhabit the world as thinkers or cognitive machines. ... My contention is that given the sorts of animals we are, we pray *before* we believe, we worship before we know—or rather, we worship *in order* to know.'[6] This seems to be in accord with what we previous observed about Hans Frei in terms of theological theory being dependent on its practice.[7] Smith is essentially applying Anselm's dictum of 'faith seeking understanding' in terms of a community-focused theology of desire as applied to our worship and educational practices, inasmuch as 'faith' involves our Christian liturgies and practices prior to our full intellectual understanding of them.

Hauerwas also agrees that we should recover the value of liturgical practices for our moral formation in the church. He submits: 'the liturgy is the necessary but not sufficient condition for the virtuous formation of our lives as Christians.'[8] The liturgical forms are indeed essential for the life and community of the Church, but he cautions against reducing liturgy to tedious, thoughtless repetition out of mere sense of duty. Simply following liturgical practices as a disengaged participant does not make one virtuous. Hauerwas points out that that Aquinas argues that virtues are gained through 'habituation of the passions'. It is not simply about merely imitating the practices of others in the community. It is not only the doing of things that shapes the mind, but a 'doing' that is not separated from the doer. As we acquire godly habits, such as acting justly, it should not only result in us doing just actions, but in our becoming just people. That is, 'you must feel what the just feel when they act justly.' Of course, this does not come instantly, but must be developed and learned, as the actions become habits. So with Hauerwas' forthright caution in mind, he eventually turns (as we noticed with Smith) to our affections. Our tastes, preferences and affections will be formed according to our virtues, but these virtues will be formed in the context of liturgical practices in the context of the Church community.[9]

As we have seen throughout this book, postliberal theology calls us away from reducing our faith to either a fundamentalist propositionalism or a liberal experientialism. Propositions always have contexts, purposes, conditions and traditions behind them. Statements of truth must be remembered in the context of flesh and blood; they stem from storied realities. If we remember this, we may be less encumbered with the burden of absolute, epistemic certainty of propositions, to humble confidence in the certainty of God who knows all. Truth will become less mathematical and more relational in tone. Rather than seeking the ever-elusive detachment of objectivity, truth will be embraced as personal and participative, as an active engagement with a person, the person of Jesus and his community of followers.[10] This is what we may call 'fleshing out' the truth. As Jesus incarnated the truth of the word to us, so we as the body of Christ today, continue to embody Jesus' as truth to others.

But we must be careful not to confuse this notion of 'fleshing it out' or incarnating the message, with a Tillichian brand of cultural accommodation. It's not about reformulating our faith in modern concepts and symbols for a new world. Instead, it is an incarnational embrace of the goodness of Creation; the embodiment of our Christian faith and practice in community as it is. In postliberal fashion, we don't simply correlate, reformat and redescribe; we teach the language of our faith and practice to the world by the practices of our faith. The grammar of this 'language' does not remain in the textbooks, pews, or ivory towers – the grammar comes to life. Jesus the word also becomes flesh in our lives.

It is also important not to confuse incarnational with fully intelligible. Jesus incarnated, but he was often misunderstood.

He nevertheless lived out his life in obedience to God; he truly embodied the Kingdom of God. This does not mean we disregard making the gospel intelligible to others in our proclamation of the gospel in words and actions. But we must realize that others' understanding will only come via the Holy Spirit's work through us as we teach the language of our faith and remain faithful to our liturgical practices in community.

Community and interpretation

We have been underlining the positive aspects of postliberal theology's chastened rationality combined with its emphasis on liturgical practices that shape our faith in community. This community centeredness, in our view, is a crucial aspect for a postliberal theological vision today, both in terms of our worship practices and our interpretation of scripture. We are the body of Christ, not individually, but corporately. A community-centred theology helps us guard against a radical individualistic self-centred Gospel that essentially has nothing to do with the Christian Gospel at all.

A postliberal theology focused on community also guards us against self-serving interpretations of the Bible used to advance our own agendas. This is not to say that particular Church communities or denominations are immune from uncharitable or self-serving interpretations. Abuses may occur corporately just as they can occur individually. But often, in our view, it is the individualistically based hermeneutic that determines that 'I' can interpret 'for me' as long as I have the Bible (which may be viewed as self-interpreting in this model). The one with the most persuasive power then becomes the theological gatekeeper for the particular community. Rather than this sort of community being based in the doctrine of the Church and its historical confessions and traditions, it often disregards these for the persuasive leader who tells us what we should believe 'now' because of his or her current interpretation of what the Bible 'says'.

In discussing future prospects for his book *The Nature of Doctrine*, in the German edition Lindbeck suggests that in theological social structures most favourable to individualism, where we find weak communal bonds, the promotion of a postliberal theology will also most likely be weak. This is especially so among 'religious people' who find it so difficult to admit that they are social creatures at the core of their being. As he puts it: 'Pietistic revivalists, old-style liberals and new age spiritualists differ on many points but not, for the most part, in their individualism and experientialism.'[11] For these 'religious people', it is often seen as contrary to religion to think of their most basic religious experiences as socially, culturally and linguistically shaped. But Lindbeck claims this is simply how scripture functions: it functions within the context of communities. Dogmatics must begin with ecclesiology and the ecclesiology of the Church cannot be separated from the narrative of Israel as the community of God. Scripture working in and through the community of God in Israel and the community of Jesus in the Church are both basic to ecumenical rethinking 'on both sides of the Atlantic'.[12] Lindbeck, as well as others holding a postliberal theological vision for the Church, emphasizes the continuity of God working through His people from all time. It is this interconnectedness of the narratives of God working through Israel and through the Church that demonstrates the ecumenical vision of the entire narrative of scripture.

Community then means more than simply 'my community' and 'my Church'. The community of the Church universal is the community of all the saints, of all God's people redeemed in Jesus. This includes our local Church community and the broader community of the body of Christ and its many manifestations, whether Methodist, Lutheran, Baptist or Roman Catholic. This is not to diminish the importance of the local Church community by any means; but the local community must locate its identity in the larger diverse community of faith universal: all God's people in the past, present and future.

We can learn from John Calvin in this respect. For Calvin, the Holy Spirit's work guiding the readers of scripture should be emphasized just as much as we stress His work guiding its authors.[13] The various theological and confessional traditions need to remain active conversation partners as we continue to offer our own confessions. This is how we maintain unity with our diversity. In the diversity of the global Church community through time, we are called to build bridges between the Spirit's activity in the past with His ongoing work in the present.[14] The larger context of the Church community was also strongly highlighted by Barth when he demanded that we listen to the theology of past periods of Church history:

> It demands a hearing as surely as it occupies a place with us in the context of the Church. The Church does not stand in a vacuum. ... We have to remember the communion of the saints, bearing and being borne by each other, asking and being asked, having to take mutual responsibility for and among the sinners gathered together in Christ. As regards theology, also, we cannot be in the Church without taking as much responsibility for the theology of the past as for the theology of our present.[15]

As we embrace the narrative of the community of God's people through history, it will help us likewise to see our connections and unity in Jesus, amidst our diversity of expressions.

As we have seen, a mark of postliberal theology is its refusal to accept the demands of modernist epistemology and historiography that either ignore or devalue tradition and community as critical to the knowing process. However, what prevents the exchange of the abandonment of modernist neutrality and replacing it with a position of assumed neutrality within the narrative itself and the community within which it is expressed? Let us explain. The postliberal theologian approaches the biblical text with full intent of shedding her modernist extra-textual ideals and practices and then turns solely toward intratextuality. However, if she believes that she can do this entirely, without any regards to those modernist influences that have shaped her life context, then she has simply replaced one assumed perspective of neutrality with another seemingly more noble perspective. The point is that we cannot escape our situatedness and context. We live in a world that often fights against such postliberal values of narrative and community. This world has influenced and does and will continue to influence how we perceive and practise intratextual ideals and proposed postliberal theological ideals. We readily agree that Enlightenment emphases of rationalism and empiricism have distorted how we should look at truth and meaning in scripture. At the same time, this 'distortion' has shaped how we think and respond in making this criticism. We simply cannot escape its formation on our thinking and actions. So rather than assume that we can fully jettison such modernist residue, in order to become presuppositionless

blank-slated beings, it would suit us better to acknowledge its
influence within the context of our community. At the same time
we must desire to move beyond modernism's imposed limitations,
continually seeking help of others to recognize how its influence
may be blinding us or preventing us from a narratival reading and
practice of scripture within the church community.

It appears that Hans Frei and David Kelsey come close to what
this criticism bemoans in advocating the descriptive or objective
work of reading scripture apart from externally imposed frameworks. Mark Alan Bowald points out that Hans Frei eventually
realized that his own distinction between meaning and truth was
'just as culpable in its heavy handed imposition of truth or explanatory schemes as those to which he was responding'. Furthermore,
Bowald continues, 'Frei also came to see that his claim about the
self-referentiality of the text was, in fact, a general theory, and
indebted to theological judgments.'[16] In our view, theological
positions cannot be avoided; it is better to acknowledge this, rather
than seek neutrality in either descriptive or normative expressions
of doctrine or theological methodology.

Let us look to another example along these lines. In his, *Proving
Doctrine: The Uses of Scripture in Modern Theology*, David
Kelsey claims that he is trying to examine theological methodologies without taking a particular theological position. With
regard to his case studies, he says that it is necessary to construe
common questions to help diagnose the cases with '"theological
position neutral" technical terms in which to state contrasting
positions fairly'.[17] It is our contention that when thinking theologically, whether in terms of methodology or in the examination of
theological methodologies, as with Kelsey's expressed intention,
that theological positions cannot be completely suppressed for the
sake of neutrality. Now in fairness, Bowald points out that Kelsey
seems to 'lapse from his theological neutrality' later in his work
when he (Kelsey) claims that decisions for the use of scripture
are indeed 'shaped by a theologian's prior judgment about how
best to construe the mode in which God's presence among the
faithful correlates with the use of Scripture in the common life
of the church'.[18] Kelsey's analysis of theological methodology
is itself dependent on theological categories pertaining to the
relationship between the participation of the reader and God's
divine agency in order to determine the meaning of scripture.[19]

Whenever we are doing theology or thinking about how we are to do theology, our reflections will always be coloured and shaped by our pre-theological notions and concerns, which are in themselves 'theological'.

But it is in the context of a diverse community of faith, with multiple voices and correctives, where the pursuit of methodological evaluation becomes more effective. Rather than presupposing a position of neutrality, we should rather presuppose a position of bias and situatedness. Our embedded positions within our cultures will at times distort and corrupt our readings and practice, but they also provide angles of access to meaning and understanding. Furthermore, realizing the snares and privileges of one's position provides a point of entry by which to access the Christian narrative within the context of a corrective community.

In addition to bringing a greatly needed reinforcement to our understanding of our global, historical Church community, postliberal theology is to be applauded for its bridge-building attempts between theologians and laity in the local Church context. As we emphasized in the introduction to this book, postliberal theology is not content to remain in academic ivory towers, but it is a theology for everyday people in the practising Church. As Douglas Okholm says, 'we can celebrate the tendency of postliberalism to wrench Scripture from the control of the academic elite and return it to the church as a world-creating and identity-forming text for the laity.'[20] Its community emphasis makes theology central to the Church rather than being reduced to an academic exercise.

In spite of the various criticisms and cautions expressed in this book, postliberal voices are to be commended for navigating Protestant theology away from the individualism that has heavily marked both liberalism and fundamentalism. It attempts to guide the individual away from focusing on oneself, back to the community of faith. At the same time, postliberal proposals challenge us with further reflection on Christian accountability as it pertains to scripture, tradition and the community of the local Church. If indeed the Bible is sovereign over the 'interpreting Church' as Barth would demand,[21] how do we read and understand the Bible apart from its interpreting community? What then is the relationship between personal accountability to the Bible and personal accountability to the community? We need the community for interpretation of the Bible and proper interpretation also depends on ecclesial practice within the community of faith. So theoretically we can affirm Barth's declaration, but applying it seems impossible apart from the practising church community.

Another question arises in view of postliberalism's ecumenical leanings with regard to the community of faith: do these reflections draw Protestant thinkers closer to or further from Roman Catholic theology? As Gabriel Fackre asks: 'Is there an *evangelical* catholicity that honors the role of the universal Christian community, its historic doctrine and even a pastoral teaching office, but holds each of these determinedly accountable to a christologically read Scripture and thus is neither awed nor tempted by the claims of Rome?'[22] Perhaps the word 'tempted' is not the word we should choose here, for it betrays a presupposition of something that may lure us away from that which is of Christ. Yet the allurement of Rome will certainly haunt Protestants who feel 'stuck' in the modernist conundrum between liberalism and fundamentalist evangelicalism. Liberalism attempted to generalize human experience at the expense of the narrative of the gospel, whereas fundamentalism has subjectivized (and often reduced) the gospel into a radically personal, individual experience. Postliberal theology does not provide all the answers to this conundrum, but it opens up a space in which such questions may be ardently pursued.

The Holy Spirit's role

Indeed, the emphasis placed on community in a postliberal vision of theology is crucial to escape the rampant individualism of Western culture. As the body of Christ, *together* we are the temple of the Holy Spirit, not individual *temples* of the Holy Spirit. But what is the place of the Holy Spirit in the narrative, preservation and spiritual health of the community? If the community is the embodiment of Jesus through the mediating work of the Holy Spirit, where is this specifically emphasized in postliberal theology? We would suggest that a more developed postliberal theology must not only emphasize community, but also fully emphasize the community as the extended narrative of the embodiment of Jesus in the world through the Holy Spirit's work within that body. It is a Holy Spirit-infused community.

With the descriptive tendencies of postliberal theology and the emphasis on theology as the grammar of the faith community, an intentional emphasis must be placed on the role of the Holy Spirit in the deciphering and transmission of this grammar to God's people for its continuity and unity. The Holy Spirit is certainly not ignored in postliberal theology, as we will highlight shortly. But the Holy Spirit's role in the community's interpretive practices of the Christian narrative should continue to be given great priority in future postliberal theological expressions.

C. C. Pecknold's research shows that the role of the Holy Spirit was certainly in Augustine's mind as he taught his readers about the signs of scripture revealed by the Holy Spirit to the community to provide healing, restoration and love. That is, the signs in scripture are incarnated in the context of community; the word is made flesh in a liturgical fashion through their performance in the Church community.[23]

William Placher effectively points out that Karl Barth presented his theological reflections on community and virtue in his *Church Dogmatics* in the context of the Holy Spirit. For Barth, the Holy Spirit continually works to unify God's people, just as He was seen with Augustine and Calvin. We are one in Christ, not as individuals, but in Christian community. For Barth, the unity we have in Christ mirrors the unity that is found in the Trinity. Additionally, for Barth, it is only through the gift of Holy Spirit, by God's grace, whereby we have access to faith and face the opportunity to know God and enjoy a transformed life.[24]

Hans Frei gave consideration to the Holy Spirit's role in interpretation in *The Eclipse of Biblical Narrative* as he hearkened back to Calvin and Luther in his discussion on precritical interpretation of scripture. The testimony of Holy Spirit was simply part of what it means to comprehend a biblical narrative. The narrative is that which provides access to the reality of the Bible and the Holy Spirit is part of the complete process of interpretation. When speaking more specifically of Calvin in this regard, Frei wrote: 'The internal testimony of the Spirit, then, is neither a peripheral edifying appendage to the actual reading of the biblical text nor an explanatory theory that alone would warrant the unity of the objective claims made in the text with the personal life stance of Christian faith.'[25] The main point is that the Holy Spirit's work is concurrent with the act of interpreting; He works in and through the interpreting process. The Holy Spirit is not separate from logic and community; He works in the midst of both. We do not abandon rationality and logic altogether in favour of a pneumatological approach to community and interpretation, but we embrace a chastened rationality that leaves room and even encourages the seeking of truth beyond mere verificationist borders. The Holy Spirit is certainly beyond modern borders of verification.

Using D. Lyle Dabney as his conversation partner, Richard Crane probes the question on the compatibility between Lindbeck's cultural–linguistic version of postliberal theology with a view of the Holy Spirit that both precedes and follows the word of God. Crane believes that Lindbeck comes dangerously close to confining the Holy Spirit's work to a cultural–linguistic paradigm, thus minimizing His sovereignty as God. Lindbeck acknowledges that the Holy Spirit enables our subjective understanding and acceptance of Christianity, but his pneumatology seems to depend on his cultural–linguistic understanding of religion more than it does on the biblical narrative itself. In contrast, Dabney refuses to suggest that the Holy Spirit is in any way related to human ability. The Spirit of God is oriented towards His word, and He orients His people towards his word. This insight is relevant for appropriations of postliberal theology in order to avoid reducing the Holy Spirit to an anthropological or cultural structure.[26]

William Placher and Bruce Marshall intentionally integrate the Holy Spirit's work into their epistemological postliberal theological paradigm. They advocate an epistemology of the Spirit, recognizing that 'knowledge' comes via the Holy Spirit through the community of Jesus. Placher claims that the Holy Spirit is too often neglected in our theology, but he insists that a strong doctrine of the Holy Spirit is necessary for a proper view of God's transcendence. Placher devotes a chapter to the place of the Holy Spirit with a postliberal theological vision. Like Barth, Placher strongly affirms that it is the Holy Spirit that reveals God's revelation in the narrative of scripture, and it is the Holy Spirit who unites us to God and with each other in community. But the Holy Spirit cannot be mastered or tamed by us; He is God, unpredictable and beyond our control. At the same time, with His untamable character, the Spirit grants us the gifts for managing the needs of the church as we serve each other in community. In fact, the Holy Spirit guides and helps shape every aspect of our Christian existence. Placher especially emphasizes, however, while drawing on the Reformed tradition (especially Calvin, Edwards, and Barth), the role of the Holy Spirit in our knowledge, love, perceptions, unity and faith.[27]

As the Holy Spirit mediates the revelation of God to us, it enables the transformation of our hearts, which, in turn, helps us to understand more about God's revelation. Our knowledge cannot be separated from our faith and actions. Understanding the narrative of scripture cannot be divorced from the cultivation of Christian practices of love. Knowledge and practice are in a continual, dialogical relationship – both of which are a result of the Holy Spirit's active work in our lives.

Placher points out that we also see this integral tie between our affections and intellect through the Holy Spirit in both Calvin and Jonathan Edwards. Edwards spoke of the 'inner testimony of the Holy Spirit' that guides us to observe things with 'excellency'. In a similar fashion, as we consider the patchwork of narratives of Jesus in the Bible, the Holy Spirit guides us to see how these patterns are reflected in God's work through His people throughout history.[28] If the community of the Church is the embodiment of Jesus with a mission to carry out the embodied ministry of Jesus, then a healthy postliberal theology would do well to strongly emphasize, as Placher as done, the Holy Spirit's presence in the interpretive work of the community, along with the Spirit's guiding and gifting for the identity and edification of the community.

Another creatively insightful work by James K. A. Smith, *Thinking in Tongues*, is highly relevant for the future of postliberal theological expressions, especially as it relates to a pentecostal worldview and spirituality.[29] Smith, staying in tune with his previous reflections noted in *Desiring the Kingdom*, proposes an 'affective, narrative epistemology' of the heart that embraces humans as narratival beings not simply as rational animals. For Smith, knowledge is 'rooted in the heart' and imagination and story precede the intellect. Smith claims that a pentecostal spirituality has an antirationalist epistemic grammar. It is not against rationality per se, but against the modern idolatrous reliance on rationality that reduces knowledge to logic, often characteristic of modernity. In this regard, a pentecostal spirituality with an affective, narrative epistemology is truly postmodern. It exposes the flaws of modernity that promoted universal reason and intellectual neutrality, both of which were shown to be veiled agendas of secularism. A postmodern vision sees a more full-orbed humanity that includes emotions, creativity, and particularity.[30] Implicit in Smith's view, and instructive for a robust postliberal theology, is a 'philosophical anthropology and epistemology that resist the slimmed-down reductionism of modern cognitivism' and hence 'fosters a more expansive, affective understanding of what counts as knowledge and a richer understanding of how we know'.[31] So Smith, like postliberal theologians, is not only repudiating modernist reductionism, he is also promoting a fuller approach to knowledge that recognizes that we are human beings who not only think, but who feel, imagine and live as 'storying' people.

It is this embodied, richer and thicker type of knowing that brings Smith to affirm an irreducible 'narrative knowledge' that draws on our emotive faculties that have shaped our under-standings of the world. Smith argues, based on his research in the social sciences, that as humans we are basically 'wired' for this way of understanding reality. With narrative knowledge, truth is the narrative; the truth is in the story – both form and content. In this regard, the 'storying' of truth is not some sort of postmodern creative option for making knowledge claims; it is absolutely essential for our humanity.[32] We are most essentially passionate beings that live and understand within our stories in community; logic and rationality are always filtered and expressed through the context of our affections.

So where does the Holy Spirit fit in all of this? The Holy Spirit is implicitly related to the embodied character of Smith's affective, narrative epistemology. The Spirit is the author and player of the entire process of coming to know. He is there as the protagonist to the entire story all the time through our desires, imagination, emotions *and* cognitions. This is not simply about opening up a richer theological epistemology and anthropology in order to make space for the Holy Spirit's work, it is about understanding that the Holy Spirit works in every aspect of our being to guide us into truth. This includes both his work of moral transformation in our lives and our narrative embodiment within the context of community.[33] So, the Holy Spirit does not simply 'fit' into a pneumatological epistemology, he is instrumental and active before, with, and through the entire process.

Smith is not a waving the 'postliberal' theological flag, but his research parallels some significant postliberal themes and, in our estimation, it helps pave the way forward for ongoing postliberal proposals. Although we would place a stronger emphasis on the head and heart dialectic than Smith may, his corrective to rationality makes a valuable contribution and provides an engaging 'antirationalist' negative and positive apologetic for postliberal theology.

Kevin Vanhoozer's 'postliberal' revision: a canonical–linguistic theology

We would be remiss not to mention Kevin Vanhoozer's work under the rubric of new proposals and prospects with regard to postliberal theology. In Vanhoozer's tome, *The Drama of Doctrine: A Canonical Linguistic Approach to Christian Theology*, he proposes a theological approach to doctrine that attempts both to maintain Lindbeck's emphasis on practising the faith, while rooting it more solidly in the scripture. He does this by encouraging a theo-dramatic approach to doctrine (*pace* Catholic theologian, Hans Urs von Balthasar), while drawing on, yet notably expanding his previous research in speech-act theory. Vanhoozer asks the question on whether, in Lindbeck's postliberal theology, doctrine stems from the narrative of scripture or from its performance in the context of community.[34] Vanhoozer sees Lindbeck's emphasis to be lopsided on the latter.

Vanhoozer also believes that Lindbeck does not do justice to the performative context of propositions. Of course, propositionalists make the same mistake by pulling propositions out of their speech-act context and hence reducing them to mere assertions. But propositions themselves are not the culprits. For Vanhoozer, both Lindbeck and propositionalists fail to see the richer value of propositions when they are used not only for stating 'facts', but for making promises, giving orders, expressing sarcasm and making jokes.[35] Vanhoozer is not making a case against Lindbeck by simply refuting his (Lindbeck's) critique of propositionalism, he is simply saying that Lindbeck's critique fails to recognize the diversity and richness of how language operates using propositions. At the same time, he would implicitly agree with Lindbeck's sentiments against propositionalism for distorting the narrative of scripture.

We have been consistently emphasizing the value of narrative in a postliberal epistemology and understanding of the Christian faith. Story is absolutely central to postliberal theology. However, Vanhoozer submits that perhaps narrative itself is not as central to Lindbeck's theology as much as his notion of theological grammar, which makes the story doctrinally normative. In other words, the Church's use of the story in its 'grammar' becomes more important that the narrative rendering of Christ. For example, what becomes most important is not the actual story of Jesus with the woman at the well, but rather the Church's use of this story in its life and practice. If this is the case, has not Lindbeck simply replaced the propositionalism and experientialism he rejected in modernism with a cultural anthropological grammar?[36] Vanhoozer wisely alerts us to the dangers of a postliberal theology (at least Lindbeck's version) that replaces propositions and experience with an overemphasis on the grammar of the community, seemingly replacing one reductionist option for another. To avoid such reductionism, Vanhoozer submits that we must look instead to the 'grammar' of God in the canon.

In view of this deficiency that Vanhoozer observes in Lindbeck's approach, he offers a performance understanding of divine discourse that keeps God front and centre in the narrative. Vanhoozer believes that Lindbeck correctly sees that language is the way we communicate in community, but he neglects to see God as the primary spokesman and author of the narrative in this linguistic community.[37] Vanhoozer claims 'the divine author is not merely a teacher who passes on propositional truths or a narrator who conveys the discourse of others but a dramatist who does things in and through the dialogical action of others'.[38] The primary difference between Lindbeck's cultural–linguistic theology and Vanhoozer's canonical–linguistic approach is the shift from the grammar of the community to the grammar of God in the 'patterns and usages' of the canon of scripture itself. God is the divine 'playwright' who uses a variety of voices to communicate scripture.[39] Hans Frei, when commenting on Karl Barth said: 'God's Word is God himself in the form of his own spiritual speech-act.'[40] Of course, God actively worked and works through the creativity of His people to perform His speech acts. God is not some detached observer who sits back and watches the play unfold; He continues to work out His ongoing drama through our human creativity both in our words and practices in and through the Church.

How then do we evaluate whether or not there is a faithful performance? Vanhoozer criticizes Lindbeck's earlier position that seemed to say that intratextuality alone was sufficient to demonstrate the faithful performance of scripture. Instead, Vanhoozer argues, Lindbeck acknowledges the need to also turn to authorial discourse and intentionality. Vanhoozer claims that it appears that Lindbeck made the move beyond a cultural–linguistic model to the canonical–linguistic approach. With the canonical–linguistic approach of Vanhoozer, normativity would not ultimately lie with the community's practice of scripture, but with God as the divine author of scripture. If this is the case, then we can perform the scripture as a necessary act of interpretation using our human creativity while being guided by the Holy Spirit.[41]

Vanhoozer's canonical–linguistic theology is thoroughly trinitarian, and strongly emphasizes the role of the Holy Spirit in the communicative and interpretive process of scripture. The Spirit is the 'literary executor' of Christ and the one who prompted the human authors 'to present Christ'. The Spirit also mediates between Christ and the Church and enables us to understand the canon of scripture by leading the Church further into the word. Where does tradition fit into the Spirit's work in the word? Tradition is the context whereby the Spirit has worked out the scripture in the life of the Church. The Church's role in 'theo-drama' is to 'suffer the effects' of scripture put into action throughout history.[42] The Spirit then preserves, guides, directs, and sustains the ongoing performative drama of the Church acting out the script of scripture. This reworking of Lindbeck's proposal, while maintaining its essential features, functions not only as charitable corrective, but also as a creative contribution to future expressions advocating the postliberal theological vision.

Guarding against a repressive community

Adonis Vidu wisely points out another potential negative tendency of postliberal theology that should be duly considered. By its full-scale rejection of the Enlightenment project and subsequent modernism, a postliberal theology may inadvertently create an equally repressive community. If the Church makes its own claims to certainty, and applies its own rules to the reading of its texts within the context of its ecclesial practices without regard to rival claims and challenges, then what prevents the Church from imposing its pre-theological positions on the text and on those seeking the Bible for answers amidst competing calls for alliances?

At one level, nothing prevents our pre-theological positions on the text except the Holy Spirit's ongoing correctives that lead us to the word of God in the context of the Church community. At the same time, the Holy Spirit may use our pre-theological positions as the means by which to access the word. The Holy Spirit works in and through our cultures, backgrounds, and contexts. As we noted earlier, this is part of the ongoing work of the Spirit through tradition and through his historic community of the Church. Just the same, Vidu's caution must not be ignored. It is possible for those experiencing a strong sense of belonging and community to come to a point where they excuse violence, oppression, suppression and manipulation, as long as it is internally 'justified' according to the accepted grammar of the community.[43] This is an issue that requires ongoing reflection for those embracing a postliberal perspective. While the desire to sustain an ecclesiologically centred approach to truth in the context of the Christian community is admired, if a particular community expression becomes a repressively sectarian, than it will not be accomplishing or promoting the narrative of Jesus. Jesus reached out to the lost, neglected, forgotten and wounded. He loved those who hated him. Jesus' story is by no means repressive, but it is a call to embrace all people from all nations into a welcoming, warming, grace-filled community. We must appropriate a thicker view of community that acknowledges the Church catholic in order to guard against such sectarian tendencies, understanding community to be both local and universal, the Church present and historical, spontaneous and traditional.

Calling for a postliberal theological hospitality

With a 'thicker' view of the community of faith, it follows that the 'way forward is to acknowledge a unity in diversity' affirming 'a

Pentecostal plurality – that enables scripture to speak on so many levels to so many different kinds of situation.' It is this 'nonreductive evangelical catholic orthodoxy' to which we must aspire.[44] We appreciate David Buschart's suggestion of 'theological hospitality' as he applies it to unity and diversity of Christian traditions. God's gift of hospitality to us is the opportunity to share community within and outside our particular context. Our particular communities of faith function 'as a home, not a fortress, from which and within which hospitality can be extended to those who are members of other communities of Christian faith, as well as those who are not members of any community of faith'.[45] Christian hospitality is not a 'fuzzy' ecumenism that erases lines and commitments to particular Christian denominations to join a pseudo- organizational unity. We cannot erase the lines and neither should we. An 'ecclesio-theological hospitality' assumes and depends on a home base from which we can extend our hospitality; it works from the position of locality and particular conviction outward.[46] Our particularity reveals our situated nature as human beings, but it also provides us an angle by which we can demonstrate charity to those outside our own traditions, realizing that we can also learn from the broader body of Christ's community.

Thomas Oden identifies this type of ecumenical hospitality as a mark of a true Spirit-led Church. The need for unity with diversity has been a challenge from the times of the early Cchurch. From the beginning, Christians were confronted with distinctive cultural differences. Hebrew Christians would not easily separate from the traditions of worship in the synagogue. Hellenistic Christians likewise would not easily accommodate to the traditions of Jewish believers. As of Paul's second missionary journey there were also geographical differences between the churches of Macedonia and those of Asia. Granted, such divisions have multiplied exponentially through time, but the point remains the same: the Church has always had significant differences, even though the Gospel has remained the same. But the Spirit-led Church can reconcile conflict and still express its oneness in Christ through its diversity of expressions. For Oden, divisiveness and sectarianism, on one hand, and syncretism, on the other, must always be avoided. Particular communities must promote an irenic, ecumenical theological hospitality that maintains communion with differing Christian traditions. This communion will not ignore or discount genuine differences, but will keep a welcoming and learning posture to those from various traditions throughout the history of the Church.[47] Oden writes: 'The church of one generation can become prisoner to the historical-cultural forms of either its own or a preceding generation and thereby deny the catholicity of the church that moves through and beyond all generations.'[48] Oden's warnings and observations are critical for a vibrant postliberal theology that carries on Lindbeck's ecumenical vision, while at the same time fostering a strong, resilient faith expression in local, particular Christian communities.

These comments may serve as a partial response to Paul J. DeHart's critique of Lindbeck's failure to adequately consider the diversity of expressions, practice and understanding of 'communal faithfulness' in the broad diversity of the larger Christian community. For DeHart, the designations of 'postliberal' ascribed to Lindbeck and Frei do not do justice to the complexities of their differences. Nevertheless, DeHart submits that the way forward echoes back to Frei: we must advocate a generous orthodoxy that faithfully witnesses to the Resurrection, while remaining committed to redescribing and correlating the resurrection within our cultural contexts. Theology is always about 'rereading' in changing contexts.[49] Although DeHart's research on these matters is exemplary, we wonder if his proposals end up conceding to the lure of cultural accommodation that the postliberal vision seeks to overcome. Unfortunately, due to the focus and space constraints of this book, we will not be able to examine DeHart's erudite scholarship and profound analysis. We must leave this for the reader's further reading and reflection.

Conclusion

Postliberal theology is bold. It flies in the face of the mentality that the church must always adapt to its host culture in order to be vibrant and real. It argues that we do not need to conform to either a hipster faith with seeker-sensitive leanings or to modern intellectualism in order to get the message. We need instead to conform to the integrity of scripture and its narrative outworking in God's community of the Church – the embodiment of Jesus Christ and His narrative to the world.

We began this book by offering basic descriptions and themes of postliberal theology, followed by a brief examination of its origin, context and reception among theological scholars. Next, we considered the philosophical, anthropological, and sociological background influences that left their mark on its development. Among these influences we noticed several common threads distinctive of the movement. Then we looked at the theological background and key theologians representative of postliberal theology, followed by a chapter devoted to various problems and criticisms. As we noted in the introduction, although it has been our desire to condense and simplify, we have also done our best to avoid superficiality and overgeneralizations where possible.

We understand and appreciate that not everyone will agree with our choices and breakdown of the authors and the particular categories we have applied to them. One of the most profound critical interlocutors with regard to postliberal theology, Paul J. DeHart, insists that the 'conceptual framework' of 'postliberal,' especially in terms of that which is commonly ascribed to Frei and Lindbeck, has 'quietly dissolved' into a collection of loose strands and diversified channels of expression. Nonetheless, DeHart admits that we can still discern a 'vague "mood" among many contemporary theologians which, consciously in most but not in all cases, resonates with the stances of Frei or Lindbeck'.[1] It is in this 'mood' where we see the broader postliberal theological vision expressed significantly in Frei, Lindbeck and Hauerwas, but also developed, extended, reified and critically adapted, by the additional authors we have only briefly considered.

It has thus been our intent to whet the reader's appetite for further investigation into the riches of postliberal theology and its importance for a recovery of ancient sources of faith. We have additionally sought to encourage a solid embrace of the scriptures and a firm commitment to the Church. We have attempted to point out as fairly as possible postliberal theology's weaknesses and strengths for Christian thought and practice today. Lastly, we have desired to maintain the original intentions of George Lindbeck, by showing how postliberal theology provides an ecumenical reparative role, but also a healing role from the abuses and misguided tendencies in both conservative fundamentalism and modern theological liberalism.

Admittedly, we have provided only a basic background to the various areas of thought responsible for the development of postliberal theology, along with making broad-stroke efforts to consider the major voices of the movement. We make no pretensions to completeness in this short book, but we trust we have provided the necessary highlights to stimulate the desire for the reader's further study.

Suggestions for further reading

Selected primary source material for postliberal theology

Hans W. Frei, *The Eclipse of Biblical Narrative: A Study in Eighteenth and Nineteenth Century Hermeneutics* (New Haven and London: Yale University Press, 1974).
—, *Types of Christian Theology* (New Haven and London: Yale University Press, 1992).
—, *The Identity of Jesus Christ* (Eugene, OR: Wipf & Stock, 1997).
Stanley Hauerwas, *A Community of Character: Toward a Constructive Christian Social Ethic* (Notre Dame, IN: University of Notre Dame Press, 1981).

—, *Unleashing the Scripture: Freeing the Bible from Captivity to America* (Nashville, TN: Abingdon, 1993).

Stanley Hauerwas and William H. Willimon, *Resident Aliens* (Nashville, TN: Abingdon, 1989).

David H. Kelsey, *Proving Doctrine: The Uses of Scripture in Modern Theology* (Harrisburg, PA: Trinity Press International, 1999).

George A. Lindbeck, *The Nature of Doctrine: Religion and Theology in a Postliberal Age* (Philadelphia, PA: Westminster Press, 1984).

—, *The Church in a Postliberal Age*, (ed.) James J. Buckley (London: SCM Press, 2002).

Bruce D. Marshall, *Trinity and Truth* (Cambridge: Cambridge University Press, 2000).

William C. Placher, *Unapologetic Theology: A Christian Voice in a Pluralistic Conversation* (Louisville, KY: Westminster John Knox, 1989).

—, *The Triune God: An Essay in Postliberal Theology* (Louisville, KY: Westminster John Knox, 2007).

Kathryn Tanner, *God and Creation in Christian Theology* (Oxford: Blackwell, 1988).

—, Theories of Culture: A New Agenda for Theology (Minneapolis. MN: Fortress, 1997).

Background sources of postliberal theology

Cultural/anthropological/sociological

Peter L. Berger, *The Sacred Canopy: Elements of a Sociological Theory of Religion* (New York: Anchor Books, 1990), Kindle edition.

Peter L. Berger and Thomas Luckmann, *The Social Construction of Reality: A Treatise in the Sociology of Knowledge* (Garden City, NY: Anchor Books, 1967).

Clifford Geertz, *The Interpretation of Cultures* (New York: Basic Books, 1973).

Philosophical

Thomas Kuhn, *The Structure of Scientific Revolutions*, 2nd edn (Chicago: University of Chicago Press, 1970).

Alasdair MacIntyre, *After Virtue: A Study in Moral Theory*, 2nd edn (Notre Dame, IN: University of Notre Dame Press, 1984).

—, *Whose Justice? Which Rationality?* (Notre Dame, IN: University of Notre Dame Press, 1988).

Ludwig Wittgenstein, *Philosophical Investigations*, trans. G. E. M. Anscombe, P. M. S. Hacker and Joachim Schulte, rev. 4th edn, (eds) P. M. S. Hacker and Joachim Schulte (Chichester: Wiley-Blackwell, 2009).

Theological

Karl Barth, *Church Dogmatics*, (eds) G. W. Bromiley and T. F. Torrance, trans. T. H. L. Parker, W. B. Johnston, Harold Knight and J. L. M. Haire, vol. 2:1 (London and New York: T&T Clark, 2004).

Paul L. Holmer, *The Grammar of Faith* (San Francisco: Harper & Row, 1978).

Introductory articles/chapters on postliberal theology

Gary Dorrien, 'The Future of Postliberal Theology', in *The Christian Century* (July 18–25, 2001).

—, 'The Origins of Postliberalism', in *The Christian Century* (July 4–11, 2001).

James Fodor, 'Postliberal Theology', in David F. Ford with Rachel Muers (eds), *The Modern Theologians: An Introduction to Christian Theology since 1918* (Malden, MA: Blackwell, 2005).

Sheila Greeve Daveney and Delwin Brown, 'Postliberalism', in Alister E. McGrath (ed.), *The Blackwell Encyclopedia of Modern Christian Thought* (Oxford: Blackwell, 1993).

George Hunsinger, 'Postliberal Theology', in Kevin J. Vanhoozer (ed.), *The Cambridge Companion to Postmodern Theology* (Cambridge: Cambridge University Press, 2003).

Timothy R. Phillips, 'Postliberal Theology', in Walter A. Elwell (ed.), *Evangelical Dictionary of Theology* (Grand Rapids, MI: Baker, 2001).

William C. Placher, 'Postliberal Theology', in David F. Ford (ed.), *The Modern Theologians: An Introduction to Christian Theology in the Twentieth Century* (Malden, MA: Blackwell, 1997).

George R. Sumner Jr, 'Postliberal Theology', in Trevor A. Hart (ed.), *The Dictionary of Historical Theology* (Carlisle and Grand Rapids, MI: Paternoster and Eerdmans, 2000).

Terrence W. Tilley, *Postmodern Theologies: The Challenge of Religious Diversity* (Maryknoll, NY: Orbis Books, 1995).

Francophone reception

Marc Boss, Gilles Emery and Pierre Gisel (eds), *Postlibéralisme? La Théologie De George Lindbeck Et Sa Réception* (Geneva: Labor et Fides, 2004).

Germanophone reception

George Lindbeck, *Christliche Lehre als Grammatik des Glaubens. Religion und Theologie in postliberalen Zeitalter*, trans. Markus Müller, intro. Hans G. Ulrich and Reinhard Hütter (Gütersloh: Kaiser, 1994). (*Note*: This is a translation with German introduction to Lindbeck's *The Nature of Doctrine*.)

Jewish reception

Steven Kepnes, Peter Ochs and Robert Gibbs, *Reasoning After Revelation: Dialogues in Postmodern Philosophy* (Boulder, CO, and Oxford: Westview Press, 1998).
Peter Ochs, *Pierce, Pragmatism and the Logic of Scripture* (Cambridge: Cambridge University Press, 1998).
Peter Ochs, *Another Reformation: Postliberal Christianity and the Jews* (Grand Rapids, MI: Baker Academic, 2012).

Roman Catholic reception

Jeffrey C. K. Goh, *Christian Tradition Today: A Postliberal Vision of Church and World*, Louvain Theological and Pastoral Monographs 28 (Leuven and Grand Rapids, MI: Peeters and Eerdmans, 2000).
John Wright (ed.), *Postliberal Theology and the Church Catholic: Conversations with George Lindbeck, David Burrell, and Stanley Hauerwas* (Grand Rapids, MI: Baker Academic, forthcoming 2012).

Critical discussions and responses to postliberal theology

Mark Alan Bowald, *Rendering the Word in Theological Hermeneutics: Mapping Divine and Human Agency* (Aldershot: Ashgate, 2007).
Robert Andrew Cathey, *God in Postliberal Perspective: Between Realism and Non-Realism* (Aldershot: Ashgate, 2009).

Paul J. DeHart, *The Trial of the Witnesses: The Rise and Decline of Postliberal Theology* (Malden, MA, and Oxford: Blackwell, 2006).

Mike Higton, *Christ, Providence and History* (London and New York: T&T Clark, 2004).

C. C. Pecknold, *Transforming Postliberal Theology: George Lindbeck, Pragmatism and Scripture* (London and New York: T& TClark, 2005).

Timothy R. Phillips and Dennis L. Okholm (eds), *The Nature of Confession: Evangelicals & Postliberals in Conversation* (Downers Grove, IL: IVP, 1996).

Adonis Vidu, *Postliberal Theological Method: A Critical Study* (Milton Keynes and Waynesboro, GA: Paternoster, 2005).

—, 'Postliberal Theological Method: A Critical Study' *European Journal of Theology* 17, 1 (2008), pp. 39–45.

Philip Ziegler, 'Review of Paul J. Dehart, *The Trial of the Witnesses: The Rise and Decline of Postliberal Theology*', *International Journal of Systematic Theology* 9, 2 (2007), pp. 222–4.

BIBLIOGRAPHY

Barth, Karl, *The Epistle to the Romans*, trans. Edwyn C. Hoskyns, 6th edn (Oxford: Oxford University Press, 1968).
—*Evangelical Theology: An Introduction* (Grand Rapids, MI: Eerdmans, 1979).
—*Church Dogmatics*, (eds) G. W. Bromiley and T. F. Torrance, trans. T. H. L. Parker, W. B. Johnston, Harold Knight and J. L. M. Haire, vol. I, II, IV (London and New York: T&T Clark, 2004).
Berger, Peter L., *The Sacred Canopy: Elements of a Sociological Theory of Religion* (New York: Open Road 2011), Kindle edition.
Berger, Peter L. and Thomas Luckmann, *The Social Construction of Reality: A Treatise in the Sociology of Knowledge* (Garden City, NY: Anchor Books, 1967).
Boss, Marc, Gilles Emery and Pierre Gisel (eds), *Postlibéralisme? La Théologie De George Lindbeck et Sa Réception* (Geneva: Labor et Fides, 2004).
Bowald, Mark Alan, *Rendering the Word in Theological Hermeneutics: Mapping Divine and Human Agency* (Aldershot: Ashgate, 2007).
Buschart, W. David, *Exploring Protestant Traditions* (Downers Grove, IL: IVP Academic, 2006).
Cathey, Robert Andrew, *God in Postliberal Perspective: Between Realism and Non-Realism* (Aldershot: Ashgate, 2009).
Cavanaugh, William T., 'The Invention of Fanaticism ', *Modern Theology* 27, 2 (2011), pp. 226–37.
Comstock, Gary, 'Two Types of Narrative Theology', *Journal of the American Academy of Religion* 55, 4 (1987).
Crane, Richard, 'Postliberals, Truth, *Ad Hoc* Apologetics, and (Something Like) General Revelation', *Perspectives in Religious Studies* 30, 1 (2003), pp. 29–53.
Daveney, Sheila Greeve and Delwin Brown, 'Postliberalism', in Alister E. McGrath (ed.), *The Blackwell Encyclopedia of Modern Christian Thought* (Oxford: Blackwell, 1993).
DeHart, Paul J., *The Trial of the Witnesses: The Rise and Decline of Postliberal Theology* (Malden, MA, and Oxford: Blackwell, 2006).

Dorrien, Gary, 'The Future of Postliberal Theology', *The Christian Century*, (July 18–25, 2001), pp. 22–9; available from http://www.religion-online.org/showarticle.asp?title=2115 (access date May 18, 2009).

—'The Origins of Postliberalism', *The Christian Century* (July 4–11, 2001), pp. 16–21; available from http://www.religion-online.org/showarticle.asp?title=2115 (access date March 8, 2010).

Eckerstorfer, Bernhard A., OSB, 'The One Church in the Postmodern World: Reflections on the Life and Thought of George Lindbeck', *Pro Ecclesia* 8, 4 (2004), pp. 399–423.

Fletcher, Jeannine Hill, 'As Long as We Wonder: Possibilities in the Impossibility of Interreligious Dialogue', *Theological Studies* 68 (2007), pp. 531–54.

Fodor, James, 'Postliberal Theology', in David F. Ford with Rachel Muers (eds), *The Modern Theologians: An Introduction to Christian Theology since 1918* (Malden, MA: Blackwell, 2005).

Ford, David F., 'Theology: A Very Short Introduction', (New York: Oxford University Press, 1999), Kindle edition.

Franke, John, *Manifold Witness: The Plurality of Truth* (Nashville, TN: Abingdon, 2009).

Frei, Hans W., *The Eclipse of Biblical Narrative: A Study in Eighteenth and Nineteenth Century Hermeneutics* (New Haven and London: Yale University Press, 1974).

—*Types of Christian Theology* (New Haven and London: Yale University Press, 1992).

—*The Identity of Jesus Christ* (Eugene, OR: Wipf and Stock, 1997).

Geertz, Clifford, *The Interpretation of Cultures* (New York: Basic Books, 1973).

Gingerich, Mark, 'The Church as Kingdom: The Kingdom of God in the Writings of Stanley Hauerwas and John Howard Yoder', *Didaskalia* 19, 1 (2008), pp. 129–43.

Goh, Jeffrey C. K., *Christian Tradition Today: A Postliberal Vision of Church and World*, Louvain Theological and Pastoral Monographs 28 (Leuven and Grand Rapids, MI: Peeters and Eerdmans, 2000).

Grenz, Stanley J., *A Primer on Postmodernism* (Grand Rapids, MI: Eerdmans, 1996).

Guarino, Thomas G., *Foundations of Systematic Theology* (London and New York: T&T Clark, 2005).

Hauerwas, Stanley, *A Community of Character: Toward a Constructive Christian Social Ethic* (Notre Dame, IN: University of Notre Dame Press, 1981).

—'The Gesture of a Truthful Story', *Theology Today* 42, 2 (1985), pp. 181–9.

—*Unleashing the Scripture: Freeing the Bible from Captivity to America* (Nashville, TN: Abingdon, 1993).

—*Performing the Faith: Bonhoeffer and the Practice of Nonviolence* (Grand Rapids, MI: Brazos, 2004).

Hauerwas, Stanley and William H. Willimon, *Resident Aliens* (Nashville, TN: Abingdon, 1989).

Higton, Mike, *Christ, Providence and History* (London and New York: T&T Clark, 2004).

Holmer, Paul L., *The Grammar of Faith* (San Francisco: Harper &Row, 1978).

Hunsinger, George, 'Beyond Literalism and Expressivism: Karl Barth's Hermeneutical Realism', *Modern Theology* 3, 3 (1987), pp. 209–23.

—'Postliberal Theology', in Kevin J. Vanhoozer (ed.), *The Cambridge Companion to Postmodern Theology* (Cambridge: Cambridge University Press, 2003).

Jenson, Robert W., 'Karl Barth', in *The Modern Theologians: An Introduction to Christian Theology in the Twentieth Century*, (ed.) David F. Ford (Malden, MA: Blackwell, 1997).

Jones, Robert P. and Melissa C. Stewart, 'The Unintended Consequences of Dixieland Postliberalism', *Crosscurrents* 55, 4 (2006), pp. 506–21.

Kelsey, David H., *To Understand God Truly: What's Theological About a Theological School?* (Louisville, KY: Westminster John Knox, 1992).

—*Proving Doctrine: The Uses of Scripture in Modern Theology* (Harrisburg, PA: Trinity Press International, 1999).

Kenneson, Philp D., 'The Alleged Incorrigibility of Postliberal Theology', in Timothy R. Phillips and Dennis L. Okholm (eds), *The Nature of Confesson: Evangelicals and Postliberals in Conversation* (Downers Grove, IL: InterVarsity, 1996).

Kraybill, Donald, 'The Amish Forgiveness', *Amish Country News* (2008); available from http://www.amishnews.com/amishforgiveness.html (access date November 11, 2011).

Kuhn, Thomas, *The Structure of Scientific Revolutions*, 2nd edn. (Chicago: University of Chicago Press, 1970).

Lauber, David, 'Yale School', in Kevin J. Vanhoozer (ed.), *Dictionary for Theological Interpretation of the Bible* (London and Grand Rapids, MI: SPCK and Baker, 2005). 859–61.

Lindbeck, George A., *The Nature of Doctrine: Religion and Theology in a Postliberal Age* (Philadelphia, PA: Westminster Press, 1984).

—*The Church in a Postliberal Age*, (ed.) James J. Buckley (London: SCM Press, 2002).

—'An Interview with George Lindbeck: Performing the Faith', *Christian Century* (November 28, 2006), pp. 28–35.

Long, D. Stephen, *Speaking of God: Theology, Language, and Truth* (Grand Rapids, MI: Eerdmans, 2009).

MacDonald, Neil B., 'Language-Game', in Kevin J. Vanhoozer (ed.), *Dictionary for Theological Interpretation of the Bible* (Grand Rapids, MI: Baker, 2005).

MacIntyre, Alasdair, *After Virtue: A Study in Moral Theory*, 2nd edn (Notre Dame, IN: University of Notre Dame Press, 1984).

—*Whose Justice? Which Rationality?* (Notre Dame, IN: University of Notre Dame Press, 1988).

Marshall, Bruce D., *Trinity and Truth* (Cambridge: Cambridge University Press, 2000).

McDermott, Gerald R., *Can Evangelicals Learn from World Religions?: Jesus, Revelation and Religious Traditions* (Downers Grove, IL: InterVarsity, 2000).

McGrath, Alister, *A Passion for Truth: The Intellectual Coherence of Evangelicalism* (Downers Grove, IL: IVP, 1996).

—*The Genesis of Doctrine* (Grand Rapids, MI, and Vancouver, BC: Eerdmans and Regent, 1997).

McLellan, David, 'Macintyre, Alistair Chalmers', in Alister E. McGrath (ed.), *The Blackwell Encyclopedia of Modern Christian Thought* (Oxford and Malden, MA: Blackwell, 1995).

Michener, Ronald T., *Engaging Deconstructive Theology* (Aldershot: Ashgate, 2007).

Miller, Ed. L. and Stanley J. Grenz, *Fortress Introduction to Contemporary Theologies* (Minneapolis, MN: Fortress, 1998).

Myers, Benjamin, 'Review of Paul J. Dehart, the Trial of the Witnesses: The Rise and Decline of Postliberal Theology', *International Journal of Systematic Theology* 9, 2 (2007).

Nelson, Derek, 'The Vulnerable and Transcendent God: The Postliberal Theology of William Placher', *Dialog: A Journal of Theology* 44, 3 (2005), pp. 273–84.

Nullens, Patrick and Ronald T. Michener, *The Matrix of Christian Ethics: Integrating Philosophy and Moral Theology in a Postmodern Context* (Colorado Springs, CO: Paternoster, 2010).

O'Laughlin, Rebecca, 'Interview with Stanley Hauerwas', *Discourse* 8, 1 (2008), pp. 19–28.

Ochs, Peter, 'Philosophic Warrants for Scriptural Reasoning', *Modern Theology* 22, 3 (2006), pp. 465–82.

Oden, Thomas C., *Systematic Theology Vol. 3: Life in the Spirit* (Peabody, MA: Hendrickson, 1970).

Okholm, Dennis L., 'Postliberal Theology', in William A. Dyrness and Veli-Matti Kärkkäinen (eds), *Global Dictionary of Theology* (Downers Grove, IL: IVP, 2008).

Pecknold, C. C., *Transforming Postliberal Theology: George Lindbeck, Pragmatism and Scripture* (London and New York: T&T Clark, 2005).

Phillips, Timothy R., 'Postliberal Theology', in Walter A. Elwell (ed.), *Evangelical Dictionary of Theology* (Grand Rapids, MI: Baker, 2001).

Phillips, Timothy R. and Dennis L. Okholm (eds), *The Nature of Confession: Evangelicals & Postliberals in Conversation* (Downers Grove, IL: IVP, 1996).

Placher, William C., 'Hans Frei and the Meaning of Biblical Narrative', *Christian Century* 106 (1989); available from http://www.religion-online.org/showarticle.asp?title=15 (access date February 9, 2012).

—*Unapologetic Theology: A Christian Voice in a Pluralistic Conversation* (Louisville, KY: Westminster John Knox, 1989).

—'Being Postliberal: A Response to James Gustafson', *Christian Century* (April 7, 1999); available from http://www.religion-online.org/showarticle.asp?title=536

—'Postliberal Theology', in David F. Ford (ed.), *The Modern Theologians: An Introduction to Christian Theology in the Twentieth Century* (Malden, MA: Blackwell, 1997).

—*The Triune God: An Essay in Postliberal Theology* (Louisville, KY: Westminster John Knox, 2007).

Shedinger, Robert F., 'Kuhnian Paradigms and Biblical Scholarship: Is Biblical Studies a Science?', *Journal of Biblical Literature* 119, 3 (2000), pp. 453–71.

Smith, James K. A., *Who's Afraid of Postmodernism? Taking Derrida, Lyotard, and Foucault to Church* (Grand Rapids, IL: Baker Academic, 2006).

—*Desiring the Kingdom: Worship, Worldview, and Cultural Formation* (Grand Rapids, MI: Baker Academic, 2009).

—*Thinking in Tongues: Pentecostal Contributions to Christian Philosophy* (Grand Rapids, MI: Eerdmans, 2010).

Springs, Jason A., 'Between Barth and Wittgenstein: On the Availability of Hans Frei's Later Theology', *Modern Theology* 23, 3 (2007), pp. 393–413.

Steinfels, Peter, 'A Bricklayer's Son: Stanley Hauerwas & the Christian Difference', *Commonweal* (2010), pp. 12–16.

Tanner, Kathryn, *Theories of Culture: A New Agenda for Theology* (Minneapolis. MN: Fortress, 1997).

Tilley, Terrence W., *Postmodern Theologies: The Challenge of Religious Diversity* (Maryknoll, NY: Orbis Books, 1995).

Tooley, Mark, 'An Honored Prophet: Stanley Hauerwas: "America's Best Theologian",' *Touchstone* 16, 3 (April 2003); available from http://touchstonemag.com/archives/article.php?id=16-03-057-r (access date January 11, 2012).

Vanhoozer, Kevin J., *The Drama of Doctrine: A Canonical Linguistic Approach to Christian Theology* (Louisville, KY: Westminster John Knox, 2005).

Vidu, Adonis, *Postliberal Theological Method: A Critical Study* (Milton Keynes and Waynesboro, GA: Paternoster, 2005).

Westphal, Merold, 'Postmodern Theology', in Edward Craig (ed.), *Routledge Encyclopedia of Philosophy* (London: Routledge, 1998), 583–6.

Wittgenstein, Ludwig, *Lectures and Conversations on Aesthetics, Psychology and Religious Belief*, ed. Cyril Barrett (Berkeley and Los Angeles: University of California Press, 1972).

—*Philosophical Investigations*, trans. G. E. M. Anscombe, P. M. S. Hacker and Joachim Schulte, rev. 4th edn (Chichester: Wiley-Blackwell, 2009).

Yong, Amos, *Beyond the Impasse: Toward a Pneumatological Theology of Religions* (Grand Rapids, MI, and Carlisle: Baker and Paternoster, 2003).

Žižek, Slavoj, 'Tolerance as an Ideological Category', *Critical Inquiry* 34 (Summer 2008), pp. 660–82.

NOTES

Chapter One

1   See George A. Lindbeck, *The Nature of Doctrine: Religion and Theology in a Postliberal Age* (Philadelphia, PA: Westminster Press, 1984), p. 7. Cf. L. Miller and Stanley J. Grenz (eds), *Fortress Introduction to Contemporary Theologies* (Minneapolis, MN: Fortress, 1998), p. 204; and 'A Panel Discussion: Lindbeck, Hunsinger, McGrath, and Fackre', in Timothy R. Phillips and Dennis L. Okholm (eds), *The Nature of Confession: Evangelicals & Postliberals in Conversation* (Downers Grove, IL: IVP, 1996), p. 246.

2   Granted, these are generalizations and tendencies. There are certainly propositionalists and biblicists who have impeccable spiritual character and manifest radical love to others. For some astute comments on these negative influences of the Enlightenment on evangelicalism, see Alister McGrath, *A Passion for Truth: The Intellectual Coherence of Evangelicalism* (Downers Grove, IL: IVP, 1996), pp. 173–9.

3   George Hunsinger, 'Postliberal Theology', in (ed.) Kevin J. Vanhoozer (ed.), *The Cambridge Companion to Postmodern Theology* (Cambridge: Cambridge University Press, 2003), pp. 42, 43.

4   See Robert Andrew Cathey, *God in Postliberal Perspective: Between Realism and Non-Realism* (Aldershot: Ashgate, 2009), p. 4. We follow the distinctions made in Paul J. DeHart, *The Trial of the Witnesses: The Rise and Decline of Postliberal Theology* (Malden, MA, and Oxford: Blackwell, 2006), p. 19. There may be times when I diverge from using the full term 'postliberal theology,' and simply write 'postliberal' or 'postliberalism'. In these cases, I am still referring to the theological usage set forth in this book.

5   In addition to these primary sources, I will be drawing on the research of Cathey, *God in Postliberal Perspective: Between Realism and Non-Realism*, pp. 5–10. In doing this, we will be selective,

merging some of the themes into one and diversifying others. We
also will not necessarily discuss these in the same order as given
by their respective authors. Cf. also C. C. Pecknold, *Transforming
Postliberal Theology: George Lindbeck, Pragmatism and Scripture*
(London and New York: T&T Clark, 2005), p. 1; Sheila Greeve
Daveney and Delwin Brown, 'Postliberalism',￼" in Alister E.
McGrath (ed.), *The Blackwell Encyclopedia of Modern Christian
Thought* (Oxford: Blackwell, 1993), p. 455; and Timothy R.
Phillips, 'Postliberal Theology', in Walter A. Elwell (ed.), *Evangelical
Dictionary of Theology* (Grand Rapids, MI: Baker, 2001).

6   McGrath, *A Passion for Truth: The Intellectual Coherence of
Evangelicalism*, p. 134. See also Timothy R. Phillips and Dennis L.
Okholm, 'The Nature of Confession: Evangelicals and Postlberals',
in Phillips and Okholm (eds), *The Nature of Confession:
Evangelicals & Postliberals in Conversation*, p. 12.

7   Cathey, *God in Postliberal Perspective: Between Realism and
Non-Realism*, p. 5; William C. Placher, 'Being Postliberal: A
Response to James Gustafson', *Christian Century* (April 7,
1999); available from http://www.religion-online.org/showarticle.
asp?title=536 (access date February 18, 2010); Timothy R. Phillips
and Dennis L. Okholm, 'The Nature of Confession: Evangelicals
and Postlberals', in Phillips and Okholm (eds), *The Nature of
Confession: Evangelicals & Postliberals in Conversation*, p.
12. William C. Placher, 'Postliberal Theology', in David F. Ford
(ed.),*The Modern Theologians: An Introduction to Christian
Theology in the Twentieth Century* (Malden, MA: Blackwell, 1997),
p. 344.

8   Phillips and Okholm, 'The Nature of Confession: Evangelicals and
Postlberals', p. 12; and Phillips, 'Postliberal Theology', p. 938.

9   Stanley Hauerwas and William H. Willimon, *Resident Aliens*
(Nashville, TN: Abingdon, 1989), p. 24.

10 Placher, 'Being Postliberal: A Response to James Gustafson'.

11 See Philp D. Kenneson, 'The Alleged Incorrigibility of Postliberal
Theology', in Timothy R. Phillips and Dennis L. Okholm (eds), *The
Nature of Confesson: Evangelicals and Postliberals in Conversation*
(Downers Grove, IL: InterVarsity, 1996), p. 95.

12 Kenneson, 'The Alleged Incorrigibility of Postliberal Theology', p. 99.

13 See again Phillips, 'Postliberal Theology', p. 938; and Daveney and
Brown, 'Postliberalism', p. 455.

14 Cathey, *God in Postliberal Perspective: Between Realism and
Non-Realism*, p. 5; and Placher, 'Postliberal Theology', pp. 344–5.

15 Cathey convincingly adds this key theme of generous orthodoxy to a list he borrows from William Placher. See Cathey, *God in Postliberal Perspective: Between Realism and Non-Realism*, p. 6. The term was adopted by Stanley J. Grenz, *Renewing the Center* (Grand Rapids, MI: Baker, 2000), Chapter 10, then again by Brian McLaren (who would be more responsible for the term's current popularity) in his book by the same name, *A Generous Orthodoxy* (Grand Rapids, MI: Zondervan, 2004).

16 Cathey, *God in Postliberal Perspective: Between Realism and Non-Realism*, p. 6.

17 Cathey, *God in Postliberal Perspective: Between Realism and Non-Realism*, p. 6. See Hans W. Frei, *Types of Christian Theology* (New Haven and London: Yale University Press, 1992), pp. 28–55. Cathey provides a helpful discussion on these types by following David Ford's summary of Frei's types in David. F. Ford, *Theology: A Very Short Introduction* (Oxford: Oxford University Press, 1999), pp. 20–9.

18 Frei, *Types of Christian Theology*, pp. 28–30; David F. Ford, *Theology: A Very Short Introduction* (New York: Oxford University Press, 1999); Cathey, *God in Postliberal Perspective: Between Realism and Non-Realism*, pp. 7–8.

19 Frei, *Types of Christian Theology*, pp. 30–4; Ford, *Theology: A Very Short Introduction*, Kindle edition; Cathey, *God in Postliberal Perspective: Between Realism and Non-Realism*, p. 8.

20 Frei, *Types of Christian Theology*, pp. 34–8; Ford, *Theology: A Very Short Introduction*; Cathey, *God in Postliberal Perspective: Between Realism and Non-Realism*, p. 8. There is much more that should be said about these theologians, but our intent is only to mention how Frei (and Ford) use these theologians to highlight these general 'types' of theology.

21 Frei, *Types of Christian Theology*, pp. 46–51; Ford, *Theology: A Very Short Introduction*.

22 Frei, *Types of Christian Theology*, pp. 38–45; and Cathey, *God in Postliberal Perspective: Between Realism and Non-Realism*, pp. 9–10.

23 See Pecknold, *Transforming Postliberal Theology: George Lindbeck, Pragmatism and Scripture*, p. 118. For example, we will be referring to British theologian David Ford. In 1994, Lindbeck's work was translated into German by Markus Müller as *Christliche Lehre als Grammatik des Glaubens. Religion und Theologie in postliberalen Zeitalter* (Gütersloh: Kaiser, 1994). For a French-speaking

appropriation of postliberal theology see Marc Boss, Gilles Emery and Pierre Gisel (eds), *Postliberalisme? La théologie de George Lindbeck et sa réception* (Geneva: Labor et Fides, 2004).

24 Bernhard A. Eckerstorfer, OSB, 'The One Church in the Postmodern World: Reflections on the Life and Thought of George Lindbeck', *Pro Ecclesia* 8, 4 (2004), pp. 399–423 (399).

25 Pecknold, *Transforming Postliberal Theology: George Lindbeck, Pragmatism and Scripture*, p. 2.

26 Dennis L. Okholm, 'Postliberal Theology', in William A. Dyrness and Veli-Matti Kärkkäinen (eds), *Global Dictionary of Theology* (Downers Grove, IL: IVP, 2008).

27 Slavoj Žižek, 'Tolerance as an Ideological Category', *Critical Inquiry* 34 (Summer 2008), pp. 660–82 (678).

28 Hunsinger, 'Postliberal Theology', p. 53. See also p. 51 where Hunsinger notes parallels between postliberal theology and contemporary epistemology. Hunsinger cites, by way of example, Victoria S. Harrison, 'Putnam's Internal Realism and von Balthasar's Epistemology', *International Journal for Philosophy of Religion* 44 (1998), pp. 67–92, especially p. 82.

29 Thomas G. Guarino, *Foundations of Systematic Theology* (London and New York: T&T Clark, 2005), p. 313.

30 See Pecknold, *Transforming Postliberal Theology: George Lindbeck, Pragmatism and Scripture*, pp. 1–2.

31 For example, Ochs was the co-general editor with Stanley Hauerwas of a series of works under the title of *Radical Traditions: Theology in a Postcritical Key*. Also see Peter Ochs, 'Philosophic Warrants for Scriptural Reasoning', *Modern Theology* 22, 3 (2006), pp. 465–82.

32 Pecknold, *Transforming Postliberal Theology: George Lindbeck, Pragmatism and Scripture*, p. 61. Pecknold devotes an entire chapter in his work to the work of Ochs. He provides his rationale for this in the first major section beginning on p. 61.

33 By way of example, Thomas G. Guarino claims that there are clear differences between the postliberal theology of George Lindbeck and Stanley Hauerwas, but 'there are also many convergences in their work'. For a great deal of Hauerwas's 'political and moral thought is based on an embrace of a neo-Barthianism similar to that of Lindbeck's. Additionally, both Hauerwas and Lindbeck are 'distrustful of universals' and consider the nonfoundationalism of Wittgenstein with high regard. In this sense, both may be considered

under the 'rubric of postliberalism'. Guarino, *Foundations of Systematic Theology*, p. 314n. 8.

Chapter Two

1 Ludwig Wittgenstein, *Philosophical Investigations*, trans. G. E. M. Anscombe, P. M. S. Hacker and Joachim Schulte, rev. 4th edn by P. M. S. Hacker and Joachim Schulte (Chichester: Wiley-Blackwell, 2009), § 23, p. 15; p. 25, § 43, 45. Cf. William C. Placher, *Unapologetic Theology: A Christian Voice in a Pluralistic Conversation* (Louisville, KY: Westminster John Knox, 1989), p. 58.

2 Wittgenstein, *Philosophical Investigations*, §332, p. 236; see also Ronald T. Michener, *Engaging Deconstructive Theology* (Aldershot: Ashgate, 2007), p. 38.

3 Neil B. MacDonald, 'Language-Game', in Kevin J. Vanhoozer (ed.) *Dictionary for Theological Interpretation of the Bible* (Grand Rapids, MI: Baker, 2005). MacDonald cites Wittgenstein's work, *Zettel*, G. E. M. Anscombe and G. H. Von Wright (eds) (Blackwell, 1981), §411. Cf. also Wittgenstein, *Philosophical Investigations*, § 116, p. 53.

4 Placher, *Unapologetic Theology: A Christian Voice in a Pluralistic Conversation*, p. 58.

5 Ludwig Wittgenstein, *Lectures and Conversations on Aesthetics, Psychology and Religious Belief*, ed. Cyril Barrett (Berkeley and Los Angeles: University of California Press, 1972), pp. 56–7.

6 Wittgenstein, *Lectures and Conversations on Aesthetics, Psychology and Religious Belief*, pp. 58–9; D. Stephen Long, *Speaking of God: Theology, Language, and Truth* (Grand Rapids, MI: Eerdmans, 2009), p. 217–18.

7 Jeannine Hill Fletcher, 'As Long as We Wonder: Possibilities in the Impossibility of Interreligious Dialogue,' *Theological Studies* 68 (2007): 531–54 (537).

8 Long, *Speaking of God: Theology, Language, and Truth*, p. 218.

9 Paul L. Holmer, *The Grammar of Faith* (San Francisco: Harper & Row, 1978), pp. 4–6.

10 Holmer, *The Grammar of Faith*, p. 102.

11 Holmer, *The Grammar of Faith*, pp. 6–9, 11, 15.

12 Holmer, *The Grammar of Faith*, p. 17.

13 Holmer, *The Grammar of Faith*, pp. 18–19.

14 Long, *Speaking of God: Theology, Language, and Truth*, p. 220.

15 Long, *Speaking of God: Theology, Language, and Truth*, pp. 221, 224.

16 Long, *Speaking of God: Theology, Language, and Truth*, p. 227.

17 See Merold Westphal, 'Postmodern Theology', in *Routledge Encyclopedia of Philosophy*, ed. Edward Craig (London: Routledge, 1998), pp. 583–6.

18 In saying this, however, we should also say that postliberal theology is more descriptive in character and motivation than it is apologetic. It is seeking to clarify the grammar of our faith internally and on its own grounds, rather than seeking a translation of faith into a contemporary way of thinking. Of course, one may argue that this, in effect, is *an apologetic* in that by denying the need for a forthright apologetic presents a variation of an apologetic itself. That is, faith is made perspicuous by its internal character, not through external demands, verifications, or evidences. By the same token, if apologetic arguments are voiced against the faith, this perspective does not deny the need to engage such problems in an ad hoc fashion, which we will consider later in the book. See James Fodor, 'Postliberal Theology', in David F. Ford with Rachel Muers (eds), *The Modern Theologians: An Introduction to Christian Theology since 1918* (Malden, MA: Blackwell, 2005), p. 231.

19 See Holmer, *The Grammar of Faith*, pp. 73–4, 184–5.

20 Holmer, *The Grammar of Faith*, p. 204. Here we may question the use of 'knowledge'. If we deny 'knowledge' to leave room for faith (Kant), then the 'leaving room' becomes a different sort of understanding without the designation of 'knowledge'. If knowledge were only that kind of understanding or apprehension of reality that comes via the sciences, then we would not properly speak of 'knowing' that a wife or husband or son indeed loves us. But knowledge does have a broader locus of meaning than that designated by the hard sciences. So, unlike Kant's dictum, it is not that Holmer's precursory postliberal theological move would deny knowledge to leave room for faith, but would submit that it is a knowledge of a different sort that is demanded by the hard sciences. This type of religious knowledge is no less rigorous in terms of commitment (in fact, it may be *more* rigorous), but merely different in terms of how it is derived.

21 Holmer, *The Grammar of Faith*, pp. 211–12.

22 David McLellan, 'Macintyre, Alasdair Chalmers', in Alister E. McGrath (ed.), *The Blackwell Encyclopedia of Modern Christian*

Thought (Oxford and Malden, MA: Blackwell, 1995), p. 359;
Alasdair MacIntyre, *After Virtue: A Study in Moral Theory*, 2nd edn
(Notre Dame, IN: University of Notre Dame Press, 1984), pp. 12,
19, 22, 60.

23 Alasdair MacIntyre, *Whose Justice? Which Rationality?* (Notre
Dame, Indiana: University of Notre Dame Press, 1988), p. 350. Cf.
also MacIntyre, *After Virtue: A Study in Moral Theory*, pp. 110–11.

24 MacIntyre, *Whose Justice? Which Rationality?*, p. 335, 352; and
Adonis Vidu, *Postliberal Theological Method: A Critical Study*
(Milton Keynes and Waynesboro, GA: Paternoster, 2005), p. 24. Cf.
George Hunsinger, 'Postliberal Theology', in Kevin J. Vanhoozer
(ed.), *The Cambridge Companion to Postmodern Theology*
(Cambridge: Cambridge University Press, 2003), p. 51.

25 MacIntyre, *After Virtue: A Study in Moral Theory*, pp. 227, 229,
240, 244.

26 MacIntyre, *After Virtue: A Study in Moral Theory*, p. 258.
MacIntrye does not simply utter a disparaging remark about
Nietzsche, but suggests his position is an honest conclusion
stemming from the acceptance of emotivism.

27 MacIntyre, *Whose Justice? Which Rationality?*, pp. 355, 350. We
will consider this point further in a later chapter looking at problems
and criticisms of postliberal theology.

28 Jeffrey C. K. Goh, *Christian Tradition Today: A Postliberal
Vision of Church and World*, Louvain Theological and Pastoral
Monographs 28 (Leuven and Grand Rapids, MI: Peeters and
Eerdmans, 2000), p. 49.

29 Goh, *Christian Tradition Today: A Postliberal Vision of Church and
World*, pp. 50–1.

30 Goh, *Christian Tradition Today: A Postliberal Vision of Church and
World*, pp. 53–7. Goh refers to MacIntyre's essay, 'Epistemological
Crises, Dramatic Narrative and the Philosophy of Science,' *The
Monist* 60 (1977), pp. 453–72; and from *Whose Justice? Which
Rationality?*, pp. 361–4.

31 MacIntyre, *Whose Justice? Which Rationality?*, p. 356; cf. Goh,
*Christian Tradition Today: A Postliberal Vision of Church and
World*, p. 57.

32 Goh, *Christian Tradition Today: A Postliberal Vision of Church and
World*, pp. 59–60.

33 Michener, *Engaging Deconstructive Theology*, p. 39–40; See
Lawrence Cahoone in his introduction to Kuhn, in *From Modernism*

to Postmodernism, p. 309; and Stanley J. Grenz, *A Primer on Postmodernism* (Grand Rapids, MI: Eerdmans, 1996), pp. 54–5; Jaco S. Dreyer, 'The Researcher: Engaged Participant or Detached Observer', *Journal of Empirical Theology*, 11/2 (1998), pp. 6–9. Cf. Thomas Kuhn, *The Structure of Scientific Revolutions*, 2nd edn (Chicago: University of Chicago Press, 1970), pp. 50–1.

34 Fletcher, 'As Long as We Wonder: Possibilities in the Impossibility of Interreligious Dialogue', pp. 540–1. See Thomas Kuhn, *The Structure of Scientific Revolutions*, 2nd edn (Chicago: University of Chicago Press, 1970), pp. 44–5, 94, 113. Cf. also Robert F. Shedinger, 'Kuhnian Paradigms and Biblical Scholarship: Is Biblical Studies a Science? ', *Journal of Biblical Literature* 119, 3 (2000), pp. 453–71.

35 Kuhn, *The Structure of Scientific Revolutions*, pp. 44–7. Kuhn refers to Michael Polanyi, *Personal Knowledge* (Chicago, 1958). For a current edition see Michael Polyani, *Personal Knowledge: Toward a Post-Critical Philosophy* (London: Routledge, 1998).

36 Fletcher, 'As Long as We Wonder: Possibilities in the Impossibility of Interreligious Dialogue', p. 541.

37 Shedinger, 'Kuhnian Paradigms and Biblical Scholarship: Is Biblical Studies a Science? ', pp. 457–8.

38 Clifford Geertz, *The Interpretation of Cultures* (New York: Basic Books, 1973), pp. 5, 20, 24, 26.

39 Geertz, *The Interpretation of Cultures*, pp. 26–7.

40 Paul J. DeHart, *The Trial of the Witnesses: The Rise and Decline of Postliberal Theology* (Malden, MA, and Oxford: Blackwell, 2006), pp. 68–9.

41 Geertz, *The Interpretation of Cultures*, pp. 109–10.

42 Geertz, *The Interpretation of Cultures*, pp. 110–12.

43 Geertz, *The Interpretation of Cultures*, p. 112.

44 Geertz, *The Interpretation of Cultures*, p. 112.

45 Geertz, *The Interpretation of Cultures*, pp. 112–13.

46 Geertz, *The Interpretation of Cultures*, pp. 119–20.

47 Geertz, *The Interpretation of Cultures*, p. 119.

48 Geertz, *The Interpretation of Cultures*, pp. 119–20, 122, 123.

49 Geertz, *The Interpretation of Cultures*, pp. 452–3; Jason A. Springs, 'Between Barth and Wittgenstein: On the Availability of Hans Frei's Later Theology', *Modern Theology* 23, 3 (2007), pp. 393–413 (403–4).

50   Peter L. Berger, *The Sacred Canopy: Elements of a Sociological Theory of Religion* (New York: Open Road, 2011), Kindle edition.

51   Berger, *The Sacred Canopy: Elements of a Sociological Theory of Religion*.

52   Peter L. Berger and Thomas Luckmann, *The Social Construction of Reality: A Treatise in the Sociology of Knowledge* (Garden City, NY: Anchor Books, 1967), pp. 1–3.

53   Berger and Luckmann, *The Social Construction of Reality: A Treatise in the Sociology of Knowledge*, p. 3 (emphasis in original).

54   Berger and Luckmann, *The Social Construction of Reality: A Treatise in the Sociology of Knowledge*, pp. 21–4. cf. also p. 186.

55   See Berger and Luckmann, *The Social Construction of Reality: A Treatise in the Sociology of Knowledge*, pp. 188–9.

56   Berger and Luckmann, *The Social Construction of Reality: A Treatise in the Sociology of Knowledge*, pp. 41–4.

57   Berger and Luckmann, *The Social Construction of Reality: A Treatise in the Sociology of Knowledge*, pp. 45–6.

58   Berger and Luckmann, *The Social Construction of Reality: A Treatise in the Sociology of Knowledge*, p. 149.

59   Berger and Luckmann, *The Social Construction of Reality: A Treatise in the Sociology of Knowledge*, p. 158.

60   Berger and Luckmann, *The Social Construction of Reality: A Treatise in the Sociology of Knowledge*, pp. 129–47.

61   C. C. Pecknold, *Transforming Postliberal Theology: George Lindbeck, Pragmatism and Scripture* (London and New York: T&T Clark, 2005), pp. 38, 129.

62   George A. Lindbeck, *The Nature of Doctrine: Religion and Theology in a Postliberal Age* (Philadelphia, PA: Westminster Press, 1984), p. 117. Also see Pecknold, *Transforming Postliberal Theology: George Lindbeck, Pragmatism and Scripture*, p. 38.

63   Pecknold, *Transforming Postliberal Theology: George Lindbeck, Pragmatism and Scripture*, pp. 39, 42–4, 46–7, 51.

64   Pecknold, *Transforming Postliberal Theology: George Lindbeck, Pragmatism and Scripture*, p. 56.

65   Pecknold, *Transforming Postliberal Theology: George Lindbeck, Pragmatism and Scripture*, p. 57.

66   Lindbeck, *The Nature of Doctrine: Religion and Theology in a Postliberal Age*, pp. 131, 132.

67 See Lindbeck, *The Nature of Doctrine: Religion and Theology in a Postliberal Age*, pp. 36, 131; Vidu, *Postliberal Theological Method: A Critical Study*, p. 2; and Gilles Emery, 'Thomas D'Aquin Postliberal?: La lecture de saint Thomas par George Lindbeck', in Marc Boss, Gilles Emery, and Pierre Gisel (eds), *Postlibéralisme? La Théologie De George Lindbeck Et Sa Réception* (Geneva: Labor et Fides, 2004), pp. 96–7. Emery's chapter is very helpful in pointing out how Lindbeck appropriates Aquinas.

68 Gary Dorrien, 'The Origins of Postliberalism', *The Christian Century* (July 4–11, 2001), pp. 16–21; available from http://www.religion-online.org/showarticle.asp?title=2115 (access date March 8, 2010).

69 See Ed. L. Miller and Stanley J. Grenz, *Fortress Introduction to Contemporary Theologies* (Minneapolis, MN: Fortress, 1998), pp. 4–5.

70 Karl Barth, *The Epistle to the Romans*, trans. Edwyn C. Hoskyns, 6th edn (Oxford: Oxford University Press, 1968), see 'The Preface to the Second Edition', p.10.

71 Robert W. Jenson, 'Karl Barth,' in David F. Ford (ed.), *The Modern Theologians: An Introduction to Christian Theology in the Twentieth Century* (Malden, MA: Blackwell, 1997), pp. 22–4; Karl Barth, *Evangelical Theology: An Introduction* (Grand Rapids, MI: Eerdmans, 1979), p. 9.

72 See Jenson, 'Karl Barth,' pp. 24–7.

73 Jenson, 'Karl Barth,' pp. 27–8.

74 Karl Barth, *Church Dogmatics*, (eds) G. W. Bromiley and T. F. Torrance, trans. T. H. L. Parker, W. B. Johnston, Harold Knight and J. L. M. Haire, vol. 2:1 (London and New York: T&T Clark, 2004), p. 15.

75 Barth, *Church Dogmatics*, vol. 2:1, p. 315.

76 Richard Crane, 'Postliberals, Truth, *Ad Hoc* Apologetics, and (Something Like) General Revelation', *Perspectives in Religious Studies* 30, 1 (2003), pp. 29–53.

77 Stanley Hauerwas and William H. Willimon, *Resident Aliens* (Nashville, TN: Abingdon, 1989), p. 24.

78 Jenson, 'Karl Barth,' p. 27.

79 Gary Dorrien, 'The Future of Postliberal Theology,' *The Christian Century* (July 18–25, 2001), pp. 22–9; available from http://www.religion-online.org/showarticle.asp?title=2115 (access date May 18, 2009).

80 Hans W. Frei, *Types of Christian Theology* (New Haven and London: Yale University Press, 1992), p. 161.

Chapter Three

1 Mike Higton, *Christ, Providence and History* (London and New York: T&T Clark, 2004), pp. 15–18.

2 William C. Placher, 'Postliberal Theology', in David F. Ford (ed.), *The Modern Theologians: An Introduction to Christian Theology in the Twentieth Century* (Malden, MA: Blackwell, 1997), p. 345; James Fodor, 'Postliberal Theology', in David F. Ford with Rachel Muers (eds), *The Modern Theologians: An Introduction to Christian Theology since 1918* (Malden, MA: Blackwell, 2005), p. 234; See also Hans W. Frei, *The Eclipse of Biblical Narrative: A Study in Eighteenth and Nineteenth Century Hermeneutics* (New Haven and London: Yale University Press, 1974), p. 130. Richard Crane, 'Postliberals, Truth, *Ad Hoc* Apologetics, and (Something Like) General Revelation', *Perspectives in Religious Studies* 30, 1 (2003), pp. 29–53 (38).

3 Frei, *The Eclipse of Biblical Narrative*, p. 130.

4 Frei, *The Eclipse of Biblical Narrative*, pp. 130–1, 133, 135. See also, Placher, 'Postliberal Theology', p. 345.

5 Placher, 'Postliberal Theology,' p. 345. Cf. Frei, *The Eclipse of Biblical Narrative*, pp. 134, 136.

6 Frei, *The Eclipse of Biblical Narrative*, p. 134.

7 Gary Dorrien, 'The Origins of Postliberalism', *The Christian Century* (July 4–11, 2001), pp. 16–21; available from http://www.religion-online.org/showarticle.asp?title=2115 (access date March 8, 2010), p. 1; Adonis Vidu, *Postliberal Theological Method: A Critical Study* (Milton Keynes and Waynesboro, GA: Paternoster, 2005), p. 48.

8 Fodor, 'Postliberal Theology', p. 235; Hans W. Frei, *Types of Christian Theology* (New Haven and London: Yale University Press, 1992), p. 161.

9 Vidu, *Postliberal Theological Method: A Critical Study*, pp. 48–9, 52; cf. Hans Frei, *The Identity of Jesus Christ* (Eugene, OR: Wipf and Stock, 1997), pp. 54–9; Frei, *The Eclipse of Biblical Narrative*, pp. 267–81.

10 Frei, *The Eclipse of Biblical Narrative*, p. 273.

11 William C. Placher, *Unapologetic Theology: A Christian Voice in a Pluralistic Conversation* (Louisville, KY: Westminster John Knox, 1989), p. 161. Placher refers his readers to Frei, *The Eclipse of Biblical Narrative*, p. 11; and *The Identity of Jesus Christ*, p. xiv.

12 Frei, *Types of Christian Theology*, pp. 13–14.

13 Frei, *Types of Christian Theology*, pp. 15–17. Frei acknowledges the influence of Paul Ricoeur as well. George Hunsinger's revision of George Lindbeck's typology is appropriate to mention here. Hunsinger submits that 'realism' is the postliberal option as opposed to literalism. Literalism implies a univocal understanding of language, whereas a Barthian analogical understanding allows for aspect of both similarity and dissimilarity between words and the objects to which they refer. See George Hunsinger, 'Postliberal Theology,' in Kevin J. Vanhoozer (ed.), *The Cambridge Companion to Postmodern Theology* (Cambridge: Cambridge University Press, 2003), p. 47.

14 Frei, *The Eclipse of Biblical Narrative*, p, 220.

15 Placher, 'Postliberal Theology,' p. 345; Frei, *Types of Christian Theology*, p. 161.

16 Frei, *Types of Christian Theology*, p. 20.

17 See Frei, *Types of Christian Theology*, p. 19. As Frei wryly recounts: 'Someone has rightly said, 'A person either has character or he invents a method', p. 19.

18 David Lauber, 'Yale School,' in Kevin J. Vanhoozer (ed.), *Dictionary for Theological Interpretation of the Bible* (London and Grand Rapids: SPCK and Baker, 2005), pp. 859–61; Timothy R. Phillips, 'Postliberal Theology,' in Walter A. Elwell (ed.), *Evangelical Dictionary of Theology* (Grand Rapids, MI: Baker, 2001); Gary Comstock, 'Two Types of Narrative Theology,' *Journal of the American Academy of Religion* 55, 4 (1987), pp. 687–717 (692–3, 697).

19 D. Stephen Long, *Speaking of God: Theology, Language, and Truth* (Grand Rapids, MI: Eerdmans, 2009), pp. 258–9. Long refers to Hans Frei, 'Theological Reflections on the Accounts of Jesus' Death and Resurrection,' in *The Identity of Jesus Christ* (Eugene, OR: Wipf and Stock, 1997), p. 104.

20 Fodor, 'Postliberal Theology', p. 235.

21 Placher, 'Postliberal Theology', p. 346. This is discussed in Frei's work, *The Identity of Jesus Christ* (Eugene, OR: Wipf and Stock, 1997); and Phillips, 'Postliberal Theology'.

22 Frei, *The Identity of Jesus Christ*, p. 114.

23 Fodor, 'Postliberal Theology', p. 235. Fodor cites Frei, *The Identity of Jesus Christ* (Philadelphia, PA: Fortress Press, 1975), pp. 4, 7.

24 Frei, *The Identity of Jesus Christ*, pp. 78–83, 86.

25 Hans Frei, *Theology and Narrative*, cited in William C. Placher,

'Being Postliberal: A Response to James Gustafson,' *Christian Century* (April 7, 1999); available from http://www.religion-online. org/showarticle.asp?title=536 (access date February 18, 2010). See also, Hans Frei, 'Response to 'Narrative Theology: An Evangelical Appraisal,' *Trinity Journal* 8 (1987), pp. 21–4 (23–4).

26 Frei, *The Identity of Jesus Christ*, pp. 87, 91–2.

27 Frei, *Types of Christian Theology*, pp. 38–40. Frei refers to Barth's *Church Dogmatics*, vol. I, part 1.

28 Frei, *Types of Christian Theology*, p. 40.

29 Frei, *Types of Christian Theology*, p. 45. See also pp. 39, 41.

30 Frei, *Types of Christian Theology*, pp. 160–1.

31 Placher, *Unapologetic Theology: A Christian Voice in a Pluralistic Conversation*, p. 161.

32 Placher, 'Postliberal Theology', p. 346. Cf. also Frei, *Types of Christian Theology*, pp. 46–55.

33 Frei, *Types of Christian Theology*, p. 161. See also Placher, 'Postliberal Theology,' pp. 346–7.

34 Jason A. Springs, 'Between Barth and Wittgenstein: On the Availability of Hans Frei's Later Theology', *Modern Theology* 23, 3 (2007), pp. 393–413 (397); Fodor, 'Postliberal Theology', p. 236.

35 Springs, 'Between Barth and Wittgenstein: On the Availability of Hans Frei's Later Theology', p. 399.

36 William C. Placher, 'Hans Frei and the Meaning of Biblical Narrative', *Christian Century* 106 (1989); available from http://www.religion-online.org/showarticle.asp?title=15 (access date February 9, 2012).

37 It is commonly assumed that Lindbeck was the first to actually use the term 'postliberal' but George Hunsinger points out that Hans Frei used the word in his doctoral dissertation in 1956. See Hunsinger, 'Postliberal Theology', p. 45. Hunsinger cites Hans W. Frei, 'The Doctrine of Revelation in the Thought of Karl Barth, 1909 to 1922: The Nature of Barth's Break with Liberalism', unpublished dissertation (Yale University, 1956), pp. 430–4, 513, 536. However, Paul J. DeHart submits that 'post-liberal' as used by Frei is essentially referring to the specific period of Neo-Orthodoxy. Paul J. DeHart, *The Trial of the Witnesses: The Rise and Decline of Postliberal Theology* (Malden, MA, and Oxford: Blackwell, 2006), p. 19n32.

38 Terrence W. Tilley, *Postmodern Theologies: The Challenge of Religious Diversity* (Maryknoll, NY: Orbis Books, 1995), p. 94;

and George A. Lindbeck, *The Church in a Postliberal Age*, (ed.) James J. Buckley (London: SCM Press, 2002), p. 197.

39   David Tracy, 'Lindbeck's New Program for Theology: A Reflection', *The Thomist* 49 (1985), pp. 460–72, cited in Crane, 'Postliberals, Truth, *Ad Hoc* Apologetics, and (Something Like) General Revelation', p. 37.

40   See Robert P. Jones and Melissa C. Stewart, 'The Unintended Consequences of Dixieland Postliberalism', *Crosscurrents* 55, 4 (2006), pp. 506–21.

41   Lindbeck, *The Church in a Postliberal Age*, p. 198.

42   George A. Lindbeck, 'An Interview with George Lindbeck: Performing the Faith', *Christian Century* (November 28, 2006), pp. 28–35.

43   Lindbeck, 'An Interview with George Lindbeck: Performing the Faith', p. 28.

44   See C. C. Pecknold, *Transforming Postliberal Theology: George Lindbeck, Pragmatism and Scripture* (London and New York: T&T Clark, 2005), pp. 16–17; and Bernhard A. Eckerstorfer, 'The One Church in the Postmodern World: Reflections on the Life and Thought of George Lindbeck', *Pro Ecclesia* 8, 4 (2004), pp. 399–423.

45   George A. Lindbeck, *The Nature of Doctrine: Religion and Theology in a Postliberal Age* (Philadelphia, PA: Westminster Press, 1984), p. 7. See also L. Miller and Stanley J. Grenz (eds), *Fortress Introduction to Contemporary Theologies* (Minneapolis, MN: Fortress, 1998), pp. 200–1.

46   Lindbeck, *The Nature of Doctrine: Religion and Theology in a Postliberal Age*, pp. 16, 51. After Lindbeck submits that this may be due to what Lonergan calls a 'systematic differentiation of consciousness', he makes the following claim: 'Both the Protestant who insists on scriptural inerrancy and the Roman Catholic traditionalist counterpart are likely to be suffering from vulgarized forms of rationalism descended from Greek philosophy by way of Cartesian and post-Cartesian rationalism reinforced by Newtonian science; but in the early centuries of the church, ontological truth by correspondence had not yet been limited to propositionalism. Fundamentalist literalism, like experiential-expressivism, is a product of modernity', p. 51. See also Miller and Grenz, *Fortress Introduction to Contemporary Theologies*, pp. 205–6.

47   Lindbeck, *The Nature of Doctrine: Religion and Theology in a Postliberal Age*, p. 16.

48 Lindbeck, *The Nature of Doctrine: Religion and Theology in a Postliberal Age*, p. 16. Lindbeck claims that this perspective is the major point of Hans Küng's assault on the doctrine of infallibility. See p. 26n3; Lindbeck, *The Nature of Doctrine: Religion and Theology in a Postliberal Age*, p. 17.

49 Placher, *Unapologetic Theology: A Christian Voice in a Pluralistic Conversation*, pp. 162–3. Cf. also Placher, 'Postliberal Theology', p. 348.

50 Lindbeck, *The Nature of Doctrine: Religion and Theology in a Postliberal Age*, pp. 17–18.

51 Lindbeck, *The Nature of Doctrine: Religion and Theology in a Postliberal Age*, pp. 32–5. Jeannine Fletcher points out that the Lindbeck 'widens the scope of Wittgenstein's "language game" (imaged as a localized context where a particular word is uttered) to accommodate the "culture" dimension of his cultural-linguistic theory of religion.' Jeannine Hill Fletcher, 'As Long as We Wonder: Possibilities in the Impossibility of Interreligious Dialogue', *Theological Studies* 68 (2007), pp. 531–4 (537). She claims, from her research, however that Lindbeck may be conflating 'language game' with 'cultural context', p. 537n23.

52 Placher, *Unapologetic Theology: A Christian Voice in a Pluralistic Conversation*, p. 163; Fletcher, 'As Long as We Wonder: Possibilities in the Impossibility of Interreligious Dialogue', pp. 536–7.

53 Lindbeck, *The Nature of Doctrine: Religion and Theology in a Postliberal Age*, pp. 35–6.

54 Lindbeck, *The Nature of Doctrine: Religion and Theology in a Postliberal Age*, p. 35.

55 Lindbeck, *The Nature of Doctrine: Religion and Theology in a Postliberal Age*, pp. 68–9. Cf. also Tilley, *Postmodern Theologies: The Challenge of Religious Diversity*, p. 97. With this in mind, George Hunsinger submits that Lindbeck's perspective may be more properly identified as *neo*liberal, rather than postliberal, since Lindbeck is redefining the nature of doctrinal propositions. See Hunsinger, 'Postliberal Theology', pp. 44–5.

56 Placher, 'Postliberal Theology,' p. 348; Dennis L. Okholm, 'Postliberal Theology', in William A. Dyrness and Veli-Matti Kärkkäinen (eds), *Global Dictionary of Theology* (Downers Grove, IL: IVP, 2008). Cf. also Tilley, *Postmodern Theologies: The Challenge of Religious Diversity*, p. 97.

57 Lindbeck, *The Nature of Doctrine: Religion and Theology in a Postliberal Age*, p. 66. See also Fodor, 'Postliberal Theology', p. 232.

58 Lindbeck, *The Nature of Doctrine: Religion and Theology in a Postliberal Age*, pp. 66–7. Also see Placher, 'Postliberal Theology', p. 348.

59 Placher, 'Postliberal Theology,' p. 347.

60 Lindbeck, *The Nature of Doctrine: Religion and Theology in a Postliberal Age*, p. 94; Tilley, *Postmodern Theologies: The Challenge of Religious Diversity*, p. 95.

61 Lindbeck, *The Nature of Doctrine: Religion and Theology in a Postliberal Age*, p. 95.

62 Lindbeck, *The Nature of Doctrine: Religion and Theology in a Postliberal Age*, p. 109n10.

63 Lindbeck, *The Church in a Postliberal Age*, p. 196.

64 Lindbeck, *The Church in a Postliberal Age*, p. 200. Lindbeck introduced his perspectives on the important connection between Israel and the Church in *The Nature of Doctrine* when he writes 'To become a Christian involves learning the story of Israel and of Jesus well enough to interpret and experience oneself and one's world in its terms', p. 34; see also p. 70n11). However, his thinking along these lines became much more developed and highlighted the decade following this initial publication.

65 Lindbeck, *The Church in a Postliberal Age*, p. 9. See also pp. 7–8.

66 Dorrien, 'The Origins of Postliberalism', p. 4.

67 Hunsinger, 'Postliberal Theology,' p. 43. Cf. Frei, *Types of Christian Theology*, pp. 42, 124–5. See also Springs, 'Between Barth and Wittgenstein: On the Availability of Hans Frei's Later Theology'. Springs wisely cautions us not to make non sequitur assumptions regarding Lindbeck's influence on Frei in his later sociological thinking, pp. 394, 408–9, and conversely, Frei's influence on Lindbeck, p. 408.

68 Frei, *Types of Christian Theology*, p. 126.

69 Frei, *Types of Christian Theology*, p. 126.

70 Fletcher, 'As Long as We Wonder: Possibilities in the Impossibility of Interreligious Dialogue', p. 541–3. Fletcher cites from Kuhn in *Structure of Scientific Revolutions*, pp. 109–10; and Lindbeck, 'The Gospel's Uniqueness: Election and Untranslatability', *Modern Theology* 13 (1997), pp. 423–50 (427).

71 Again, see Fletcher, 'As Long as We Wonder: Possibilities in the Impossibility of Interreligious Dialogue', pp. 543–9.

72 Rebecca O'Laughlin, 'Interview with Stanley Hauerwas', *Discourse* 8, 1 (2008), pp. 19–28.

73 O'Laughlin, 'Interview with Stanley Hauerwas'.

74 Mark Tooley, 'An Honored Prophet: Stanley Hauerwas: "America's Best Theologian"', *Touchstone* 16, 3 (April 2003); available from http://touchstonemag.com/archives/article. php?id=16-03-057-r (access date January 11, 2012). See also Peter Steinfels, 'A Bricklayer's Son: Stanley Hauerwas & the Christian Difference', *Commonweal*, May 7, 2010 (2010), pp. 12–16.

75 Tooley, 'An Honored Prophet: Stanley Hauerwas: "America's Best Theologian"'.

76 See Placher, 'Postliberal Theology', p. 349; Fodor, 'Postliberal Theology', p. 236; Miller and Grenz, *Fortress Introduction to Contemporary Theologies*, p. 208. Hauerwas, a long-time Methodist theologian, now worships at an Episcopal church. Also see Fodor, 'Postliberal Theology', p. 236; Jones and Stewart, 'The Unintended Consequences of Dixieland Postliberalism', p. 508.

77 Stanley Hauerwas, *A Community of Character: Toward a Constructive Christian Social Ethic* (Notre Dame, IN: University of Notre Dame Press, 1981), pp. 37, 42–3, 45, 49, 51. Hauerwas draws from Hans Frei, *The Identity of Jesus Christ* (Philadelphia: Fortress Press, 1975) pp. 65, 59.

78 Hauerwas, *A Community of Character: Toward a Constructive Christian Social Ethic*, p. 37. See also Placher, *Unapologetic Theology: A Christian Voice in a Pluralistic Conversation*, p. 164.

79 Hauerwas, *A Community of Character: Toward a Constructive Christian Social Ethic*, p. 52.

80 Stanley Hauerwas, *Performing the Faith: Bonhoeffer and the Practice of Nonviolence* (Grand Rapids, MI: Brazos, 2004), pp. 136–7.

81 Hauerwas, *Performing the Faith: Bonhoeffer and the Practice of Nonviolence*, p. 139. Hauerwas is also careful to acknowledge that the Bible contains more genres than simply narrative (i.e. the Psalms, wisdom literature, etc.), but he believes the narrative of the Bible provides the context by which this other material becomes intelligible, pp. 138–9.

82 See Mark Gingerich, 'The Church as Kingdom: The Kingdom of God in the Writings of Stanley Hauerwas and John Howard Yoder', *Didaskalia* 19, 1 (2008), pp. 129–43. (134–5, 139); Stanley Hauerwas, 'The Gesture of a Truthful Story', *Theology Today* 42, 2 (1985), pp. 181–9.

83 Hauerwas, 'The Gesture of a Truthful Story', p. 185.

84 Placher, *Unapologetic Theology: A Christian Voice in a Pluralistic Conversation*, p. 164. Placher cites from Stanley Hauerwas and William Willimon, 'Embarrassed by God's Presence', *The Christian Century* 102 (January 30, 1985), p. 98; and Placher, 'Postliberal Theology,' p. 349; Hauerwas, *Performing the Faith: Bonhoeffer and the Practice of Nonviolence*, pp. 140–1. Hauerwas refers to Alasdair MacIntyre, *After Virtue: A Study in Moral Theory*, 2nd edn (Notre Dame, IN: University of Notre Dame Press, 1984), pp. 208, 218, 221.

85 Stanley Hauerwas, *Unleashing the Scripture: Freeing the Bible from Captivity to America* (Nashville, TN: Abingdon, 1993), pp. 18, 35, 17, 27.

86 Hauerwas, *Unleashing the Scripture: Freeing the Bible from Captivity to America*, p. 27.

87 Vidu, *Postliberal Theological Method: A Critical Study*, pp. 33–4. Cf. Hauerwas, *A Community of Character: Toward a Constructive Christian Social Ethic*, p. 60.

88 Comstock, 'Two Types of Narrative Theology', p. 704.

89 Patrick Nullens and Ronald T. Michener, *The Matrix of Christian Ethics: Integrating Philosophy and Moral Theology in a Postmodern Context* (Colorado Springs, CO: Paternoster, 2010), pp. 127–8. While Hauerwas submits that Christian ethics is distinctive, he is careful to say that this does not render his arguments exempt from outside challenges since 'arguments are arguments'. See Hauerwas, *A Community of Character: Toward a Constructive Christian Social Ethic*, p. 2. He further adds: 'My insistence on the distinctiveness of Christian ethics is not meant to be defensive or exclusionary, but derives from a frank, and I hope honest, recognition that, methodologically, ethics and theology can only be carried out relative to a particular community's convictions', p. 2; Hauerwas, *A Community of Character: Toward a Constructive Christian Social Ethic*, p. 129.

90 Hauerwas, *A Community of Character: Toward a Constructive Christian Social Ethic*, p. 3.

91 Hauerwas, *A Community of Character: Toward a Constructive Christian Social Ethic*, p. 84; and Hauerwas, *Performing the Faith: Bonhoeffer and the Practice of Nonviolence*, pp. 148–9. Hauerwas refers to both Aristotle and Aquinas as theologians who argued for the acquisition of virtues through habitual action. For

Aquinas, this was particularly important for the 'habituation of the passions'. Hauerwas, *Performing the Faith: Bonhoeffer and the Practice of Nonviolence*, p. 156; Nullens and Michener, *The Matrix of Christian Ethics: Integrating Philosophy and Moral Theology in a Postmodern Context*, pp. 127–9. See pp. 129–30 for a brief critique of Hauerwas on these points.

92 Placher, *Unapologetic Theology: A Christian Voice in a Pluralistic Conversation*, p. 163; David Kelsey, *To Understand God Truly: What's Theological About a Theological School?* (Louisville, KY: Westminster John Knox, 1992), pp. 218–19.

93 This book was republished as: David H. Kelsey, *Proving Doctrine: The Uses of Scripture in Modern Theology* (Harrisburg, PA: Trinity Press International, 1999).

94 DeHart, *The Trial of the Witnesses: The Rise and Decline of Postliberal Theology*, p. 25.

95 DeHart, *The Trial of the Witnesses: The Rise and Decline of Postliberal Theology*, pp. 27–8.

96 Kelsey, *Proving Doctrine: The Uses of Scripture in Modern Theology*, pp. 89–91, cf. pp. 97–8. Cf. Placher, *Unapologetic Theology: A Christian Voice in a Pluralistic Conversation*, p. 163.

97 See Kelsey, *Proving Doctrine: The Uses of Scripture in Modern Theology*, pp. 90–1, 109; DeHart, *The Trial of the Witnesses: The Rise and Decline of Postliberal Theology*, p. 28; Vidu, *Postliberal Theological Method: A Critical Study*, p. 35.

98 Kelsey, *Proving Doctrine: The Uses of Scripture in Modern Theology*, pp. 109–10.

99 Kelsey, *Proving Doctrine: The Uses of Scripture in Modern Theology*, p. 111.

100 Placher, *Unapologetic Theology: A Christian Voice in a Pluralistic Conversation*, p. 164; and Lauber, 'Yale School.'

101 Kelsey, *Proving Doctrine: The Uses of Scripture in Modern Theology*, pp. 92–4.

102 Kelsey, *Proving Doctrine: The Uses of Scripture in Modern Theology*, p. 94.

103 Placher, 'Being Postliberal: A Response to James Gustafson'.

104 Derek Nelson, 'The Vulnerable and Transcendent God: The Postliberal Theology of William Placher', *Dialog: A Journal of Theology* 44, 3 (2005), pp. 273-84. Nelson also quotes from William C. Placher et al., *Struggling with Scripture* (Louisville:

Westminster John Knox, 2002), p. 33. See also Placher, 'Being Postliberal: A Response to James Gustafson'.

105   Placher, 'Being Postliberal: A Response to James Gustafson'.

106   William C. Placher, *The Triune God: An Essay in Postliberal Theology* (Louisville, KY: Westminster John Knox, 2007), p. ix.

107   Placher, *The Triune God: An Essay in Postliberal Theology*, pp. 81, 92, 93, 95–9, 102–3.

108   Placher, *The Triune God: An Essay in Postliberal Theology*, pp. 129, 140, 150, 151.

109   Nelson, 'The Vulnerable and Transcendent God: The Postliberal Theology of William Placher', p. 276.

110   See Bruce D. Marshall, *Trinity and Truth* (Cambridge: Cambridge University Press, 2000), pp. xi, 3.

111   Marshall, *Trinity and Truth*, pp. 7–9.

112   Gary Dorrien, 'The Future of Postliberal Theology', *The Christian Century* (July 18–25, 2001), pp. 22–9, available from http://www.religion-online.org/showarticle.asp?title=2115 (access date May 18, 2009). Cf. Marshall, *Trinity and Truth*, pp. 54ff.

113   Marshall, *Trinity and Truth*, p. 48.

114   Marshall, *Trinity and Truth*, pp. 278–82, esp. pp. 280–1.

115   Marshall, *Trinity and Truth*, pp. 141–3, 145, 168–9.

116   Again see Marshall, *Trinity and Truth*, p. 280.

117   See, for example, George Hunsinger, *Disruptive Grace: Studies in the Theology of Karl Barth* (Grand Rapids, MI: Eerdmans, 2000).

118   Hunsinger, 'Postliberal Theology,' p. 46. The article he was referring to is George Hunsinger, 'Beyond Literalism and Expressivism: Karl Barth's Hermeneutical Realism', *Modern Theology* 3, 3 (1987), pp. 209–23.

119   Hunsinger, 'Beyond Literalism and Expressivism: Karl Barth's Hermeneutical Realism', pp. 209–11.

120   Hunsinger, 'Beyond Literalism and Expressivism: Karl Barth's Hermeneutical Realism', pp. 209–16.

121   Hunsinger, 'Beyond Literalism and Expressivism: Karl Barth's Hermeneutical Realism', pp. 212, 220.

122   Hunsinger, 'Beyond Literalism and Expressivism: Karl Barth's Hermeneutical Realism', pp. 219, 222n20.

123   Hunsinger, 'Beyond Literalism and Expressivism: Karl Barth's Hermeneutical Realism', pp. 219–20.

124 Kathryn Tanner, *Theories of Culture: A New Agenda for Theology* (Minneapolis. MN: Fortress, 1997), pp. 37–8, 40–41; Dorrien, 'The Future of Postliberal Theology'.

125 Tanner, *Theories of Culture: A New Agenda for Theology*, pp. 67, 69, 70.

126 Tanner, *Theories of Culture: A New Agenda for Theology*, p. 70.

127 Again see Kelsey, *Proving Doctrine: The Uses of Scripture in Modern Theology*, pp. 109–110.

128 Tanner, *Theories of Culture: A New Agenda for Theology*, p. 143.

129 Tanner, *Theories of Culture: A New Agenda for Theology*, p. 152, 153.

130 Tanner, *Theories of Culture: A New Agenda for Theology*, pp. 174–5.

131 Dorrien, 'The Future of Postliberal Theology'.

132 Fodor, 'Postliberal Theology', p. 350.

133 Vidu, *Postliberal Theological Method: A Critical Study*, pp. 31–3.

134 Philp D. Kenneson, 'The Alleged Incorrigibility of Postliberal Theology', in Timothy R. Phillips and Dennis L. Okholm (eds), *The Nature of Confesson: Evangelicals and Postliberals in Conversation* (Downers Grove, IL: InterVarsity, 1996), p. 103; and John Milbank, *Theology and Social Theory: Beyond Secular Reason* (Oxford: Blackwell, 1990), p. 388.

135 This is found in their book, *Truth in Aquinas* (London: Routledge, 2001); Fodor, 'Postliberal Theology', pp. 240–1.

Chapter Four

1 See Jeffrey Hensley, 'Are Postliberals Necessarily Antirealists? Reexamining the Metaphysics of Lindbeck's Postliberal Theology', in Phillips and Okholm (eds), *The Nature of Confession: Evangelicals & Postliberals in Conversation*, pp. 71–2. Hensley gives examples of this antirealist reading of postliberal theology from evangelical theologians Donald Bloesch and Alister McGrath, along with evangelical philosopher Thomas Morris. However, Hensley also points out that this criticism is not unique to evangelicals. See p. 72, comments in n. 9.

2 Timothy R. Phillips, 'Postliberal Theology', in Walter A. Elwell (ed.), *Evangelical Dictionary of Theology* (Grand Rapids, MI: Baker, 2001).

3   See Pecknold, *Transforming Postliberal Theology: George Lindbeck, Pragmatism and Scripture*, p. 8.

4   Hensley, 'Are Postliberals Necessarily Antirealists?', p. 74.

5   Hensley, 'Are Postliberals Necessarily Antirealists?', pp. 73–4.

6   Hensley, 'Are Postliberals Necessarily Antirealists?', pp. 78, 80.

7   Comstock, 'Two Types of Narrative Theology', p. 694; Long, *Speaking of God: Theology, Language, and Truth*, p. 241. Long also cites Fergus Kerr with reference to Wittgenstein, in *Theology after Wittgenstein* (Oxford: Blackwell, 1986), p. 131.

8   Crane, 'Postliberals, Truth, *Ad Hoc* Apologetics, and (Something Like) General Revelation', Crane describes Marshall's distinction and claims that Lindbeck has indeed endorsed Marshall's depiction as an accurate reflection of his own position. See Bruce Marshall, 'Aquinas as Postliberal Theologian', and George Lindbeck, 'Response to Bruce Marshall', *The Thomist* 53 (1989), pp. 354–406.

9   George Hunsinger, 'What Can Evangelicals & Postliberals Learn From Each Other?: The Carl Henry-Hans Frei Exchange Reconsidered', in Phillips and Okholm (eds), *The Nature of Confession: Evangelicals & Postliberals in Conversation*, p. 146.

10 Long, *Speaking of God: Theology, Language, and Truth*, pp. 296–302, 318.

11 Comstock, 'Two Types of Narrative Theology', p. 694.

12 Alister E. McGrath, *The Genesis of Doctrine* (Grand Rapids, MI, and Vancouver, BC: Eerdmans and Regent, 1997), pp. 33–5.

13 McGrath, *The Genesis of Doctrine*, pp. 38–40, 34.

14 Placher, *Unapologetic Theology: A Christian Voice in a Pluralistic Conversation*, pp. 131–2.

15 Crane, 'Postliberals, Truth, *Ad Hoc* Apologetics, and (Something Like) General Revelation', p. 41.

16 Frei, *The Identity of Jesus Christ*, pp. 57–9.

17 Frei, *The Identity of Jesus Christ*, p, 58.

18 Frei introduced this idea in reference to Barth. See Frei, *Types of Christian Theology*, p. 161. This was then philosophically developed by William Werpehowski, 'Ad hoc Apologetics', *Journal of Religion* 66, 3 (1986), pp. 282–301.

19 Placher, *Unapologetic Theology: A Christian Voice in a Pluralistic Conversation*, p. 167. Also Frei, *Types of Christian Theology*, p. 161.

20 Dorrien, 'The Origins of Postliberalism', p. 5.

21 Lindbeck, *The Nature of Doctrine: Religion and Theology in a Postliberal Age*, p. 129. See also Fletcher, 'As Long as We Wonder: Possibilities in the Impossibility of Interreligious Dialogue', p. 544.

22 George Lindbeck, 'A Panel Discussion', in Phillips and Okholm (eds), *The Nature of Confession: Evangelicals & Postliberals in Conversation*, p. 252.

23 Lindbeck, *The Nature of Doctrine: Religion and Theology in a Postliberal Age*, pp. 129–30.

24 Lindbeck, *The Nature of Doctrine: Religion and Theology in a Postliberal Age*, pp. 130–31.

25 Lindbeck, *The Nature of Doctrine: Religion and Theology in a Postliberal Age*, pp. 131–2.

26 Lindbeck, *The Nature of Doctrine: Religion and Theology in a Postliberal Age*, pp. 132–3.

27 Terrance Tilley with Stuart Kendall, in Tilley, *Postmodern Theologies: The Challenge of Religious Diversity*, pp. 96–100.

28 Fletcher, 'As Long as We Wonder: Possibilities in the Impossibility of Interreligious Dialogue', pp. 549, 553–4.

29 Alasdair MacIntyre, *Whose Justice? Which Rationality?* (Notre Dame, IN: University of Notre Dame Press, 1988), pp. 350–1, 52–3.

30 MacIntyre, *Whose Justice? Which Rationality?*, pp. 360–1.

31 MacIntyre, *Whose Justice? Which Rationality?*, p. 359.

32 MacIntyre, *Whose Justice? Which Rationality?*, p. 360.

33 Amos Yong, *Beyond the Impasse: Toward a Pneumatological Theology of Religions* (Grand Rapids, MI, and Carlisle: Baker and Paternoster, 2003), p. 56.

34 Gerald R. McDermott, *Can Evangelicals Learn from World Religions?: Jesus, Revelation and Religious Traditions* (Downers Grove, IL: InterVarsity, 2000), p. 10.

35 See Kenneson, 'The Alleged Incorrigibility of Postliberal Theology', pp. 99–100. Kenneson also cites Stanley Fish, 'Change', in *Doing What Comes Naturally: Change, Rhetoric and the Practice of Theory in Literary and Legal Studies* (Durham, NC: Duke University Press, 1989), p. 148; see also McDermott, *Can Evangelicals Learn from World Religions?: Jesus, Revelation and Religious Traditions*, p. 18.

36 Barth, *Church Dogmatics*, IV.3.1., p. 97. See McDermott, *Can Evangelicals Learn from World Religions?: Jesus, Revelation and Religious Traditions*, pp. 108–9.

37   Barth, *Church Dogmatics*, IV.3.1., p. 97.

38   McDermott, *Can Evangelicals Learn from World Religions?: Jesus, Revelation and Religious Traditions*, p. 109. McDermott cites George Hunsinger, *How to Read Karl Barth: The Shape of His Theology* (New York: Oxford University Press, 1991), pp. 61–2.

39   Placher, *Unapologetic Theology: A Christian Voice in a Pluralistic Conversation*, pp. 168–9.

40   Hauerwas, *A Community of Character: Toward a Constructive Christian Social Ethic*, p. 37.

41   Placher, *Unapologetic Theology: A Christian Voice in a Pluralistic Conversation*, pp. 164–5.

42   Placher, *Unapologetic Theology: A Christian Voice in a Pluralistic Conversation*, p. 169.

43   Placher, *Unapologetic Theology: A Christian Voice in a Pluralistic Conversation*, p. 167; also Daveney and Brown, 'Postliberalism'.

44   Donald Kraybill, 'The Amish Forgiveness', *Amish Country News* (2008); available from http://www.amishnews.com/amishforgiveness. html (access date November 11, 2011).

45   Donald Kraybill, 'The Amish Forgiveness'.

46   Tanner, *Theories of Culture: A New Agenda for Theology*, p. 152.

47   Fodor, 'Postliberal Theology', p. 236.

48   Mike Higton, *Christ, Providence and History* (London and New York: T&T Clark, 2004), pp. 1–2.

49   Kenneson, 'The Alleged Incorrigibility of Postliberal Theology', p. 102.

50   Kenneson, 'The Alleged Incorrigibility of Postliberal Theology', p. 105.

Chapter Five

1   James K. A. Smith, *Who's Afraid of Postmodernism? Taking Derrida, Lyotard, and Foucault to Church* (Grand Rapids, MI: Baker Academic, 2006), pp. 136–7.

2   William T. Cavanaugh, '"The Invention of Fanaticism'," *Modern Theology* 27, 2 (2011), pp. 226–37 (227).

3   Cavanaugh, 'The Invention of Fanaticism'. He develops this argument fully in his book, *The Myth of Religious Violence: Secular*

Ideology and the Roots of Modern Conflict (New York: Oxford University Press, 2009).

4   James K. A. Smith, *Desiring the Kingdom: Worship, Worldview, and Cultural Formation* (Grand Rapids, MI: Baker Academic, 2009), p. 25.

5   Smith, *Desiring the Kingdom: Worship, Worldview, and Cultural Formation*, pp. 24–5.

6   Smith, *Desiring the Kingdom: Worship, Worldview, and Cultural Formation*, p. 34.

7   Frei, *Types of Christian Theology*, p. 19.

8   Hauerwas, *Performing the Faith: Bonhoeffer and the Practice of Nonviolence*, p. 160.

9   Hauerwas, *Performing the Faith: Bonhoeffer and the Practice of Nonviolence*, pp. 158, 160–1.

10 Rodney Clapp, 'How Firm a Foundation: Can Evangelicals Be Nonfoundationalists?,' in Phillips and Okholm (eds), *The Nature of Confession: Evangelicals & Postliberals in Conversation*, p. 92.

11 George A. Lindbeck, *The Church in a Postliberal Age*, James J. Buckley (ed.) (London: SCM Press, 2002), p. 199.

12 Lindbeck, *The Church in a Postliberal Age*, p. 200.

13 Placher, *The Triune God: An Essay in Postliberal Theology*, p. 94. Placher points this out and cites from Calvin, *Institutes* 3.2.33; 1.580–81; and 1.7.4; 1.79.

14 John Franke, *Manifold Witness: The Plurality of Truth* (Nashville, TN: Abingdon, 2009), pp. 35–6.

15 Karl Barth, *Protestant Theology in the Nineteenth Century*, new edn (Grand Rapids, MI: Eerdmans, 2002), p. 3 cited in Franke, *Manifold Witness: The Plurality of Truth*, p. 36.

16 Mark Alan Bowald, *Rendering the Word in Theological Hermeneutics: Mapping Divine and Human Agency* (Aldershot: Ashgate, 2007), p. 89.

17 Kelsey, *Proving Doctrine: The Uses of Scripture in Modern Theology*, pp. 2, 7–9.

18 Kelsey, *Proving Doctrine: The Uses of Scripture in Modern Theology*, p. 167; Bowald, *Rendering the Word in Theological Hermeneutics: Mapping Divine and Human Agency*, p. 92. Bowald also cites Kelsey from above text.

19 Bowald, *Rendering the Word in Theological Hermeneutics: Mapping Divine and Human Agency*, p. 92.

20   Okholm, 'Postliberal Theology'.

21   See Gabriel Fackre, 'Narrative: Evangelical, Postliberal, Ecumenical',
     in Phillips and Okholm (eds), *The Nature of Confession:
     Evangelicals & Postliberals in Conversation*, pp. 129–30.

22   Gabriel Fackre, 'Narrative: Evangelical, Postliberal, Ecumenical', p. 130.

23   Pecknold, *Transforming Postliberal Theology: George Lindbeck,
     Pragmatism and Scripture*, pp. 55–7.

24   Placher, *The Triune God: An Essay in Postliberal Theology*, pp. 108–11.

25   Frei, *The Eclipse of Biblical Narrative*, p. 24.

26   Crane, 'Postliberals, Truth, *Ad Hoc* Apologetics, and (Something Like)
     General Revelation', pp. 46–7, 49–50. See also Lindbeck, *The Nature
     of Doctrine: Religion and Theology in a Postliberal Age*, p. 34.

27   See Placher, *The Triune God: An Essay in Postliberal Theology*,
     pp. ix, 84–92, 109; see also Marshall, *Trinity and Truth*, pp. 278–82.

28   Placher, *The Triune God: An Essay in Postliberal Theology*, pp. 93–9,
     102–108.

29   See James K. A. Smith, *Thinking in Tongues: Pentecostal
     Contributions to Christian Philosophy* (Grand Rapids, MI:
     Eerdmans, 2010). The small 'p' in pentecostal is intentional in
     Smith's work, as he is not referring 'to a classical or denominational
     definition, but rather to an understanding of Christian faith that is
     radically open to the continued operations of the Spirit', p. xvii.

30   Smith, *Thinking in Tongues: Pentecostal Contributions to Christian
     Philosophy*, pp. 43–4, 53–9.

31   Smith, *Thinking in Tongues: Pentecostal Contributions to Christian
     Philosophy*, p. 59.

32   Smith, *Thinking in Tongues: Pentecostal Contributions to Christian
     Philosophy*, pp. 63–7.

33   Smith, *Thinking in Tongues: Pentecostal Contributions to Christian
     Philosophy*, pp. 63, 67–9.

34   Kevin J. Vanhoozer, *The Drama of Doctrine: A Canonical Linguistic
     Approach to Christian Theology* (Louisville, KY: Westminster John
     Knox, 2005), pp. xiii, 17, 171.

35   Vanhoozer, *The Drama of Doctrine: A Canonical Linguistic
     Approach to Christian Theology*, pp. 278–9.

36   Vanhoozer, *The Drama of Doctrine: A Canonical Linguistic
     Approach to Christian Theology*, pp. 172, 175. Vanhoozer's
     critique seems to voice a similar concern we suggested earlier with
     the tendency for postliberal theological voices to overly accentuate

theological description, as we noted especially when discussing the work of David Kelsey.

37 Vanhoozer, *The Drama of Doctrine: A Canonical Linguistic Approach to Christian Theology*, pp. 176–7.

38 Vanhoozer, *The Drama of Doctrine: A Canonical Linguistic Approach to Christian Theology*, p. 179.

39 Vanhoozer, *The Drama of Doctrine: A Canonical Linguistic Approach to Christian Theology*, p. 213.

40 Frei, *Types of Christian Theology*, p. 159.

41 Vanhoozer, *The Drama of Doctrine: A Canonical Linguistic Approach to Christian Theology*, pp. 183–5. Vanhoozer refers to George Lindbeck, 'Postcritical Canonical Interpretation: Three Modes of Retrieval', in Christopher R. Seitz and Kathryn Greene-McCreight (eds), *Theological Exegesis: Essays in Honor of Brevard S. Childs* (Grand Rapids, MI: Eerdmans, 1999).

42 Vanhoozer, *The Drama of Doctrine: A Canonical Linguistic Approach to Christian Theology*, pp. 198–9, 201–3.

43 Vidu, *Postliberal Theological Method: A Critical Study*, p. 43.

44 Vanhoozer, *The Drama of Doctrine: A Canonical Linguistic Approach to Christian Theology*, p. 275.

45 W. David Buschart, *Exploring Protestant Traditions* (Downers Grove, IL: IVP Academic, 2006), p. 263.

46 Buschart, *Exploring Protestant Traditions*, pp. 262–3, 266–7, 269.

47 Thomas C. Oden, *Systematic Theology Vol. 3: Life in the Spirit* (Peabody, MA: Hendrickson, 1970), pp. 311–12.

48 Oden, *Systematic Theology Vol. 3: Life in the Spirit*, p. 313.

49 Benjamin Myers, 'Review of Paul J. DeHart: *The Trial of the Witnesses: The Rise and Decline of Postliberal Theology*', *International Journal of Systematic Theology* 9, 2 (2007), pp. 222–4. Paul J. DeHart, *The Trial of the Witnesses: The Rise and Decline of Postliberal Theology* (Malden, MA and Oxford: Blackwell, 2006); Myers, "Review of Paul J. DeHart: *The Trial of the Witnesses: The Rise and Decline of Postliberal Theology*' pp. 54, 168, 182–4, 235, 279.

Conclusion

1 DeHart, *The Trial of the Witnesses: The Rise and Decline of Postliberal Theology*, pp. 43–4.

INDEX OF AUTHORS

SUBJECT INDEX